Taylor Swift

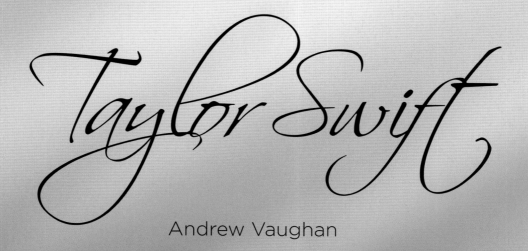

Taylor Swift

Andrew Vaughan

STERLING

New York

STERLING
New York

An Imprint of Sterling Publishing
387 Park Avenue South
New York, NY 10016

ISBN 978-1-4027-8812-3

Distributed in Canada by Sterling Publishing
c/o Canadian Manda Group, 165 Dufferin Street
Toronto, Ontario, Canada M6K 3H6
Distributed in the United Kingdom by GMC Distribution Services
Castle Place, 166 High Street, Lewes, East Sussex, England BN7 1XU
Distributed in Australia by Capricorn Link (Australia) Pty. Ltd.
P.O. Box 704, Windsor, NSW 2756, Australia

Produced for Sterling Publishing by Essential Works
www.essentialworks.co.uk

Publishing Director: Mal Peachey
Managing Director: John Conway
Editors: Lori Paximadis & Nicola Hodgson
Designer: Michael Gray

For information about custom editions, special sales, and premium and corporate purchases,
please contact Sterling Special Sales at 800-805-5489 or specialsales@sterlingpublishing.com.

Manufactured in the United States of America

2   4   6   8   10   9   7   5   3

www.sterlingpublishing.com

CONTENTS

INTRODUCTION

How did a teenage girl sell millions of albums and singles, rack up more than 30 million downloads as one of the biggest-selling digital artists in popular music history (in the process amassing millions of Facebook, Twitter, and MySpace supporters), sell out whole tours in hours at prestigious concert venues, become the CMA's youngest ever Entertainer of the Year, and pick up a cool four Grammy awards on one night, all before turning twenty–one?

I'm thankful to have been in the right place at the right time on a couple of occasions to witness at close hand the careers of two other country music super-stars who shook the industry to the core and changed the way it presented itself and, more significantly, its perception around the world. My fledgling music critic career happened to coincide with Garth Brooks coming to Nashville and estab-lishing himself as a superstar. I was one of the first international journalists to interview him, long before he had a number one–selling record. Our paths crossed on many occasions, and I was able to witness a genuine musical superstar as he learned how not only to play the country music game, but change most of the rules and practically revolutionize the genre by himself. Some years later I was fortunate to spend time with a young Shania Twain, an eager and enthusiastic artist, keen to help promote country music to new markets with my then employer Country Music Television (Europe). Shania had trouble being accepted by the country music community, perhaps because as a Canadian she really was an outsider, or maybe because they simply weren't ready for her sexy midriff-baring image at a time when Nashville was more conservative than it is today.

I certainly didn't think I'd see their like again. So when I started hearing word of a young girl from Hendersonville, a small town north of Nashville, who was building an army-sized fan base on the Internet, it a seemed like an interesting story, but probably just a novelty.

Every year in March, country music's most powerful radio executives gather in Nashville for Country Radio Seminar. Naturally, the country music record companies, major and independent, take this opportunity to woo, cajole, per-suade, and entice radio's movers and shakers to listen to, and hopefully play, their new artists' music. It's a time to consolidate relationships for the big names and a massive opportunity to showcase new talent.

Nobody grabbed the attention of the industry audience in 2008 like the tall young blonde wearing a short minidress who was singing and dancing her way through an intense high-energy performance of pop country. Once they saw her in action, whether on stage or relating with the fans and the media, suddenly the predictions that Nashville had a new star in the making made sense. For many this was their first exposure to Taylor Swift, the highlight of 2008's CRS New Faces series. "Different," "energetic," "feisty," "promising writer," "breath of fresh air," they muttered in the darkened hotel ballroom.

It was a breath of fresh air indeed for a country music industry that was perilously close to falling into recession. Country music in the mid–2000s needed an injection of new life. Record sales were down, and around the CRS convention halls media pundits talked about country music lagging behind the technological revolution in music and lacking the necessary talent to keep young people inter-ested. While *American Idol* had given country music Carrie Underwood, it was still unclear how genuine a country artist she would become, or be allowed to become, in Nashville, which is partly is why people were talking about Taylor Swift. She was young, Internet savvy, already popular, and—significantly for a town that under-stands the power of the songwriter—wrote her own songs.

As a new singer, an aura of mystique developed around this girl from Hendersonville who had millions of Internet fans. Some people thought she was the best thing since Shania—a songwriter with an innate pop sensibility who was going to break through bigger than anyone before her. A few labeled her lightweight teen froth. How wrong they were. This book tells Taylor's story in the context of the country music world she revolutionized and looks at how she managed to make it when so many fail to make an impression. I wanted to show the effect she had on country music at a time when the business was facing some serious challenges.

Her story, and those of those around her, is fascinating. Taylor, whether consciously or subconsciously, tapped into a new market. Country music had neglected a whole sector of the record-buying public in the new millennium. As the Internet forced record stores out of business and the album market dipped, pop music discovered a new market of teen sensations. Young Disney acts like Miley Cyrus sold CDs by the million in the face of a worldwide economic recession. And then there were downloads, the new digital currency of music. Country music was lagging significantly behind there, and it hadn't seriously considered an audience so young as potential fans of their kind of artists.

Taylor's confessional, underdog-oriented adolescent love songs struck a chord with young girls across America. Her experiences were their experiences. Her brilliantly produced and immaculately performed songs are autobiographical, honest, naïve, angry, exuberant, catchy, and sad in equal measure. Taylor Swift understands the teenage victim of bullying because she was one. She knows how it feels to suffer unrequited love and be unceremoniously dumped by a lover. Awkwardness, rejection, teen crushes, love, and pain—that's what Taylor expressed, and it was what her fans knew and felt.

NO FENCES

Not since Garth Brooks has an artist enjoyed such a close relationship with her audience. Honest and open to a fault, Taylor's constant blogging made her an Internet superstar. She posted, commented, laughed, and cried online and interacted with a whole generation of fans. She was honest with her fans. Her Internet posts and songs were like pages from her diary. And she understood, intuitively, the power of relating to her audience and interacting with them. Her blog posts were not the typical news announcements that other, older, stars allowed their record companies to post for them; hers were calls to action, gossipy girl chat, and ongoing dialogue with kids just like herself. If it had been premeditated it would have been brilliant. But it wasn't planned, just wonderfully executed.

Nashville was quick to get behind the teen phenomenon. Taylor was smart, beautiful, charming, gifted, and obviously possessed of the necessary will to succeed. After coming late to the Shania party, the industry, especially the CMA, was determined to acknowledge and embrace the Swift hurricane as it gathered velocity. Taylor Swift wasn't going to wait years for their validation, so they gave her their biggest award, Entertainer of the Year, while she was still a teenager.

Swift has made the most of her talents. She paid her dues from age ten onward with trips to Nashville from her home state of Pennsylvania, developing her skills and learning the industry game as she grew up. While other kids were goofing off, Taylor Swift was writing songs, rehearsing, and recording—and picking up straight A's at school. Like Garth Brooks and Shania Twain before her, Taylor values her opportunities and works incessantly to achieve new goals. When she moved out of her family home she could have bought a palace in the hills like most of her peers. But not Taylor. Instead, she purchased a condo in a luxury building smack bang in the middle of Music Row, just a stone's throw from the wonderfully named Chet Atkins Avenue.

Above all, perhaps, Taylor is a great songwriter. She's won the prestigious NSAI songwriter/artist award three times (at the time of writing), and when no less an authority on the art of the song than legendary country music maverick Kris Kristofferson praises her writing, it reflects that Nashville respects Taylor as a writer. And as everyone in Music City knows, it all begins with a song.

Like Garth, Shania, and the Dixie Chicks before her, Taylor has not blinked an eye at taking on the world. Taylor is as at home on stage at a rock festival in England or chatting about fashion to a French TV host as she is calling in and thanking radio stations in Iowa for playing her music. Taylor Swift, to the fans around the world, is a music star. Period.

Country music, in Taylor Swift's unaffected and charming hands is—finally—cool for kids everywhere. It couldn't have happened with less design, less orchestration, or manipulation. One of the best songwriters to surface in years, her rise to the top has been rapid, dramatic, and fascinating to witness. Something tells me that there will be many more chapters written about Taylor Swift's entertainment career, whether that is in country music or pop and rock, on TV or in movies. But that's another story.

Andrew Vaughan
March 2011

1

A Place in this World

TAYLOR Swift entered the world at Reading Hospital in Reading, Pennsylvania just before Christmas in 1989. And it wasn't a bad time to make her mark. The U.S. economy grew rapidly through the 1990s. The old enemy, the Soviet Union, was finally gone, and with America enjoying the fruits of a technology boom, the economy grew substantially. Low inflation was good for corporate America, and healthy profits sent the stock market through the roof. The Dow Jones Industrial average, by which economists measure economic performance, went from 1,000 in the 1970s to 11,000 in 1999. It was a good time for Taylor Swift's father, Scott, to be a stockbroker. If money had been tighter, perhaps Swift's parents might have been less likely to indulge their daughter's dreams and be supportive while she pursued her career.

Nashville, a city that would play such a significant part in Taylor Swift's journey, also benefited from a strong economy. In the year Taylor was born Garth Brooks released his self-titled debut album and enjoyed a couple of hits; his next two albums changed the nature of country music forever.

Thanks to Brooks and later Shania Twain, country music, so often associated only with southern and western America, became a truly global phenomenon. Twain would sell 39 million copies of her album *Come on Over* worldwide. Brooks and Twain, besides crossing genres and national borders, took control of their own careers, making business decisions and, significantly, writing much of the music that put them on the map. They would prove to be great role models indeed for Taylor Swift, an innately curious quick learner who loved music.

There was nothing especially remarkable about Taylor Swift's childhood and early years in rural Pennsylvania, except perhaps the way she handled childhood adversities and developed an incredibly self-assured will to succeed. Taylor, unlike many other country music superstars before her, had no outwardly obvious hurdles to get over. She didn't grow up in a one-room shack, like Dolly Parton did; she wasn't married at age thirteen, like Loretta Lynn was; and she didn't have to raise her brothers and sisters by herself, like Shania Twain did.

But Taylor Swift had her own issues to deal with, issues facing the modern girl in a MySpace world, and she handled them all with uncommon grace and necessary defiance. On the surface everything in Swift's childhood was wonderful. Her parents were well off financially. She lived in beautiful rural Pennsylvania on a Christmas tree farm (her father's other business) but was close enough to the local town and shopping malls to feel connected with the modern world.

HOME ON THE CHRISTMAS TREE FARM

It was somehow fitting that the young Taylor, born on December 13, 1989, would be raised on a Christmas tree farm. As she told Jay Leno on *The Tonight Show*: "I was too young to help with the hauling of the trees up the hills and putting them onto cars. So, it was my job to pull off the praying mantis pods from the Christmas trees. The problem with that is if you leave them on there, people bring them into their house. I forgot to check one time and they hatched all over these people's house. And there were hundreds of thousands of them. And they [the family] had little kids, and they couldn't kill them because that'd be a bad Christmas."

Hard work and family values were instilled in Taylor at a young age by her parents and her teachers at the Alvernia Montessori School, where she attended preschool and kindergarten. The school director, Sister Ann Marie Coll, told the *Reading Eagle* newspaper, "She was kind of shy, but not too shy, and she always liked to sing. When she was in grade school, she came back and played guitar for the children."

There was little drama at home for Taylor and her younger brother, Austin, and life looked just about as perfect and American pie as it gets. But as Taylor grew into a curious and driven child with her own individual interests and passions, she felt

PREVIOUS PAGES: Taylor at the Roberto Cavalli fashion show in Milan, September 2010.

OPPOSITE: A stylish Taylor arriving at the 2008 American Music Awards in L.A.

different than other kids around her, and small-town America has never been particularly fond of much that is different. Taylor Swift was bullied and ostracized in school, making her preteen and early teen years tough to bear, which is why music was so important to her. Music provided her with an outlet for her inner pain and a means to change her life. Ironically, though, it was her love of music, originally inspired by hearing LeAnn Rimes when she was just six years old, that would drive a wedge between Taylor and other girls in her community.

"If I had been popular I wouldn't have wanted to leave"

For the most part, home life in Wyomissing, in Berks County, Pennsylvania, was safe and comfortable. Taylor's father was a successful stockbroker, and her mother, Andrea, was also in finance until she quit working to be a stay-at-home mom. Just to add a little glamour to the mix, Taylor's grandmother was a renowned opera singer. In her early years Taylor was just like everyone else. She attended school and played with the local kids. Summers were spent by the beach at Stone Harbor in New Jersey, where she loved to indulge in her favorite pizza at the Italian Garden restaurant on 96th Street or cookies 'n' cream ice cream at Springers. Like any kid her age, she also spent hours creating her own entertainment. As she told the *Philadelphia Inquirer*:

It was really cool living on the bay, and we have so many stories about it. We used to all gather together on the dock when the boat parades would go by on July 4 and we'd shoot water balloons at them.

I made a clubhouse in the room above my garage and made a filing system of members of the club. Everyone had a profile that I would write on tiles I found. I painted the whole room different colors and used to spend all day in there just doing nothing but sitting in my little club.

We lived across from the bird sanctuary and I had a pair of binoculars, and some days I'd just stare at the window, looking for birds. Or the boy who lived next door to me, whom I swore I would marry someday. One summer when I was 11, I wrote a novel. I was allowed to be kind of weird and quirky and imaginative as a kid, and that was my favorite part of living at the Shore.

OVERTURE

As a kid, Taylor, like many of her contemporaries, gravitated toward music, especially Disney tunes. Taylor's mother told the *Press of Atlantic City*, "Taylor has been singing constantly since she could talk. We would take her to a movie like the *Little Mermaid* and she would memorize the songs right away and sing them on the way home." She just loved music. Her father's parents had been musicians, and her grandmother on her mother's side was Marjorie Findlay, an acclaimed opera singer who influenced Taylor. Taylor told *CMT Insider*: "My grandmother was an opera singer, and so she was always singing, either around the house, or every single Sunday she'd get up and sing in front of the entire congregation at church."

In January 1996, thirteen-year-old LeAnn Rimes released her debut album. When six-year-old Taylor heard LeAnn Rimes and recognized that the singer was still a child herself, she was captivated. Subsequently Taylor gravitated toward country music, listening in particular to LeAnn, Shania Twain, and the Dixie Chicks. (Her very first demo tape includes a version of LeAnn Rimes's song "One Way Ticket.")

Swift told the *Guardian* newspaper: "LeAnn Rimes was my first impression of country music. I got her first album when I was six. I just really loved how she could be making music and having a career at such a young age.

"Ever since I discovered their music I wanted to do country music. I wanted to sing country music. Didn't matter if I lived in Pennsylvania. Didn't matter if everybody at my school was like, 'You—you? Play country music? Why do you like country music? You're so weird.'"

It was taking shape, a love of country music, a discovery or a talent for writing, a love of English at school, and a natural affinity with performing. She told New Zealand's *3 News*, "Music was what I loved and writing was what I loved. I always looked forward to English class; I think I was the only kid who was like, Yes! Creative writing!" When she was in fourth grade, at age nine, Taylor entered a national poetry contest and won it with her poem "Monster in My Closet."

Perhaps like most kids, Taylor loved to perform. She started doing karaoke when she was ten at Henry's Restaurant in Stone Harbor, New Jersey. She threw herself into acting, starting off with a school play performance in second grade.

"I knew I wanted to act and sing when I was in that play," she said. "Right after that, I saw an ad for a children's theater company and I auditioned. I got in the company, and in my second play I got a lead role. I love singing more than acting but I like to act because I think it helps with stage presence."

"Hi, I'm Taylor. I'm 11; I want a record deal. Call me."

Taylor Swift, with her singing voice and height giving her natural advantages over some of her contemporaries, played the lead on several kids' productions, including Sandy in *Grease*, Kim in *Bye Bye Birdie*, and Maria in *The Sound of Music*. These experiences gave Swift an audience for her karaoke performances at the productions' after-show parties. Singing her favorite country music tunes by LeAnn Rimes, Shania Twain, and Faith Hill to her peers and their parents, the Taylor Swift blueprint for success was being drawn.

PESTER POWER!

One day when Taylor was ten years old, she sat at home watching a profile of country music superstar Faith Hill on TV. She later told the UK's Paul O'Grady: "When I was ten I saw this TV program about Faith Hill. And it said when Faith Hill was nineteen or so she moved to Nashville and that's how she got into country music. So I had this epiphany when I was ten. 'I need to be in Nashville—that's a magical dream world where dreams come true.' So that's when I started on my daily begging rant. Eventually they took me on a trip there when I was eleven."

In the meantime, Taylor's ever supportive parents happily traipsed around the state with their talented daughter, entering karaoke contests and visiting fairs and events where there was a chance she could sing and perform. In March 2001, when Taylor was eleven, her constant badgering to go to Nashville finally paid off. Andrea Swift gladly, if cautiously, took her daughter to Nashville, Tennessee, the spiritual and physical home of the country music industry, for a quick visit.

Taylor told *Blender* magazine about the innocent naïveté of the first trip to Music City. "I had a demo CD of me singing karaoke music. We rented a car, and we would pull up in front of a label on Music Row and I'd walk in and talk to the receptionist: 'Hi, I'm Taylor. I'm eleven. I really want a record deal.'"

BELOW LEFT: A young Taylor
during her high school
years and performing
at Hendersonvile High
School in 2006.

There can't be too many cities in the world where a sensible mother would feel comfortable letting her eleven-year-old walk into record company building alone with her demo tape and a smile. Certainly not in London, New York, or Los Angeles. But Nashville remains a friendly, hospitable, and welcoming city, and Taylor was not alone in knocking on doors. Workers on Nashville's famous Music Row (an area around Sixteenth and Seventeenth Avenues south of downtown, where all kinds of companies in the record business have offices) are used to dealing with a parade of wannabes knocking on doors and hoping their dreams will be fulfilled by the star makers in Music City. Every week hundreds walk the streets of Music Row: tourists one minute, new talent the next. Taylor may have been younger than many, but the sales pitch and the offering up of a demo tape were things the receptionists were more than used to. In fact, many of the receptionists on Music Row are themselves undiscovered singers and songwriters, waiting for their chance to slip a demo tape to the right executive. They call it the "Nashville handshake" in Music City, the subtly palmed demo tape offered to anyone who might help a career take off. Taylor—although not yet a teenager—had a remarkable sense that the music business was where she wanted to be and demonstrated an uncanny understanding of how it worked. Instead of being deterred by discovering that she wasn't the only new talent looking for a deal in 2001, she worked on giving herself an advantage, an edge over the competition when it came time to be taken seriously.

As she told *CMT Insider*, "After the trip that we initially took and met with people on Music Row, I went home and decided that I needed to learn a few more things before I went back. I learned guitar and I learned songwriting, and I never put it down."

Taylor Swift's guitar playing had a fortuitous beginning when a computer repairman working at the Swift family home announced that he could play a little. Taylor immediately asked him to show her a few chords, and he taught her the basic three: A, D, and E. Taylor, ever the determined overachiever, practiced those three chords for hour after hour till her fingers bled. She was intent on mastering the instrument in order to have another string to her bow. She knew at eleven that being a singer wasn't enough for Nashville; she needed to be a songwriter, which she became when she wrote her first song with those first three chords, "Lucky You."

Aside from normal things like schoolwork, Taylor devoted her life to finding places to sing and play. She also came up with the smart idea of singing at sporting events locally. She told *Rolling Stone*: "It occurred to me that the National Anthem was the best way to get in front of a large group of people if you don't have a record deal." Starting locally, Swift was soon singing the national anthem at every place that would have her and that she could fit into her increasingly hectic schedule. The policy paid off when she was invited to sing the national anthem at the US Open tennis tournament in New York. It was there that she was spotted by a music artist manager named Dan Dymtrow, who was then manager of Britney Spears. Impressed by young Taylor and convinced he could do something with her, Dymtrow signed Swift and soon would open several doors for her in what proved to be the short period they worked together.

ABOVE: Having hit the big time, Taylor performs during the Fearless Tour at a sold-out Madison Square Garden, New York, in 2009.

PLUGGING AWAY

Unfortunately, Taylor's local successes didn't make her any friends at Wyomissing Area Junior Senior High School. Her mother explained to E's *True Hollywood Story* that jealousies arose every time Taylor received some fame and attention. "I knew that if she sang the national anthem for the 76ers and it was in the newspapers, it was going to be a tough day at school." Taylor had some heartbreaking situations to handle but found a way of putting the bullying into perspective and to good use, too. She told E's *True Hollywood Story*: "In middle school I had to deal with a situation where I would literally walk up and sit down at a lunch table full of girls and they would all get up and leave as soon as I sat down. I could take what happened that day that was horrible, and turn it into something good. I can write songs and that's where I could be happy."

BELOW: Backstage at the Grammy Awards, Los Angeles, in 2008.

Taylor Swift was never one to sit and wait for others to create opportunities for her. Not only did she sing at every sporting event she could, she used her newfound guitar abilities to perform even more shows in the Reading area. She told *CMT Insider*: "So instead of playing at karaoke bars and things like that where I needed to drag my little karaoke machine everywhere, I would go with my guitar and I would plug it in at coffeehouses, and I would bring my little amplifier and plug it in at Boy Scout meetings. I would plug it in at all these different places, little random places where you could play. I now had a portable instrument, and I could go accompany myself, and I could play anywhere I wanted to. That really expanded the places where I could play and my abilities. I played so much that I came a long way in a short period of time."

The difference in the twelve-year-old Taylor who began making regular trips to Nashville with her parents and the naïve girl with a karaoke demo tape was huge. She had learned to play the guitar, in the process discovering a rare ability to combine her love of poetry with her newly found guitar skills to write simple but touching three-minute country songs. She told *CMT Insider*: "When I was about twelve, we started going to Nashville and taking trips every two months or so, going to Nashville for a week trying to meet songwriters, trying to get my foot in the door at different places. Eventually, we scored this meeting with RCA Records when I was thirteen. I went into RCA, and I pulled out my guitar and I played them a bunch of songs, maybe twenty songs. The A&R people there said, 'We want to sign you to a development deal.' And that was when I was thirteen. A development deal is not a full-on record deal. It's not 'All right, we're going to make an album. Let's go.' It's 'We're going to sponsor and pay for your demos that you do over this next year, and we're going to see how you grow as an artist. And then in a year, we're going to decide whether we want you or whether we want to develop you for more time or whether we want to drop you.' It's a noncommittal commitment, but I was elated. I was just, 'Oh, my gosh! This huge record label wants to sign me to a development deal! I'm so excited!' So we started coming to Nashville more and more and more, and eventually we just decided to move."

Andrea Swift, looking back on the RCA development deal, told E's *True Hollywood Story* about how the company's belief in her daughter's abilities gave the Swift family faith that their daughter did in fact have what it takes to make it in the world of the music business. She said, "Okay, so I'm not crazy. I'm not just a bad parent, and there's a real validation there."

Not far from where Taylor lived in Pennsylvania, a local country music singer named Pat Garrett ran weekly karaoke contests at his Garrett Roadhouse in Strausstown. Garrett was as close to a country music star, with his own record label, as anything in the Swifts' part of Pennsylvania, and not only did Taylor enter his contests regularly, but her father, Scott, pumped Garrett for information and advice as to how to best nurture his precociously talented daughter and give her the greatest possible chance of success in the music business. Garrett told *CBS News* about his encounters with the young country singer and how he advised Scott to take Taylor to Nashville. "Her dad showed me a notebook she had, and in this ring notebook the only thing she had was her signature, practicing her autograph. She has an insatiable drive."

On one occasion Scott Swift dropped by Garrett's sheepskin store to ask him about what he should do with Taylor. Garrett told him that to make it in country music you have to go to Nashville. Given that Garrett was better informed about the music business, and country music in particular, Scott Swift gave his recommendations some serious thought.

Garrett said, "Three months later he comes in my store, the sheepskin store, and says, 'Well, we're going,' and I said, 'Well, that's nice. How long you going for?' figuring he's going for three weeks. He said, 'The rest of our lives.'"

"My father had a job he could do from anywhere," Swift told *Blender* magazine. "My parents moved across the country so I could pursue a dream."

THE DIXIE CHICKS

TEXAS'S super successful all–female Dixie Chicks were one of ten-year-old Taylor Swift's favorite groups, and she'd always sing along to them at her karaoke nights. She even included her own version of the Dixie Chicks' "There's Your Trouble" track on the demo CD that first began to get her noticed in Nashville.

While the Chicks seemed to appear from nowhere in 1998, playing a fiery brand of bluegrass, country, and rock that music fans immediately warmed to, they had in fact been paying their dues and learning their craft in Texas for almost ten years.

The original lineup didn't feature the singer who made them famous (and some might say, infamous), Natalie Maines. They began as a four piece in Dallas, Texas, with Emily and Martie Erwin, joined by Laura Lynch and Robin Macy. In 1992 Macy quit because she wanted to play purer bluegrass than the Chicks were writing, and in 1995 Lynch left to spend more time with her family. Natalie Maines was recruited as the Dixie Chicks' new singer.

Sony loved the more commercial sound that Maines brought to the band and signed them to their revamped Monument label, releasing their stunning debut album, *Wide Open Spaces*, in 1998. Their first single, "I Can Love You Better," made the top 10 while the next three, "There's Your Trouble," "Mine," and the title track, "Wide Open Spaces," were all country number ones. The Chicks appealed to all music lovers, it seemed, not just country fans. They had worked at broadening their appeal. One of their first tours was on the mostly rock- and pop-inclined Lilith Fair extravaganzas, and that exposed them to a predominantly non-country audience. Taylor cannot have failed to notice how the Chicks sold more albums that year than all the other country acts together: that was the power of broader musical horizons.

The Chicks' next album, *Fly*, released in 1999, continued the good work the first album had started, with more hits, and by 2003 the Dixie Chicks were the highest-grossing touring act in country music. Once on top, however, the band began to have problems. First they fell into dispute with their record company, Sony, whom they accused of withholding royalties via some incorrect accounting practices. They sued, settled out of court, and started their own Open Wide Records with Sony handling distribution.

But that was a minor hiccup compared to the storm that was about to blow across the Atlantic. It all started in London, England, in March 2003, just days before the United States'-led invasion of Iraq. Natalie Maines was none too happy about her country's planned military action that night. Speaking from the stage of London's Shepherd's Bush Empire, the Texan Maines said: "Just so you know, we're on the good side with y'all. We do not want this war, this violence, and we're ashamed that the president of the United States is from Texas."

Once her statement made it into the *Guardian* newspaper's live review, it spread across the Internet like a virus. Many conservative media commentators in America were angered by Maines's statement, and thousands of country fans were hurt and outraged by it. Fans in America boycotted Dixie Chicks shows and even destroyed their albums in public displays of protest and anger. Disturbingly, the trio also faced several death threats.

Madonna and Bruce Springsteen spoke out publicly in their defense, but public opinion was seemingly against them. When Maines next became embroiled in a war of words with fellow country singer Toby Keith, the Dixie Chicks' days as major league stars looked to be over. In 2006, however, they came back with a new record, *Taking the Long Way*, which won them five Grammy awards, including Best Record, Best Album, and Best Song ("Not Ready to Make Nice"). However, Nashville and country radio were not yet ready to forgive and forget. Taylor never stopped being a fan, it seems, and, if nothing else, she learned from them not to mix politics with pleasure. Sure, she'll promote a good cause such as a charity, but Taylor is unlikely to ever speak out on anything controversial in public.

Country music loves and respects Taylor (look at her award count!) and it's hard to imagine fans ever destroying a Taylor Swift album or radio stations banning her, even if she does share certain qualities with the Chicks—namely writing great songs and refusing to be confined by genres and formula.

OPPOSITE: The Dixie Chicks in 2006, from left to right, Emily Robison, Natalie Maines, and Martie Maguire.

2

Missing

N Los Angeles, movie stars live in palaces and castles that sit in the Hollywood Hills, high above the city. In London, superstars keep residences in swanky parts of town like Kensington and Chelsea or buy houses in the lush, leafy countryside surrounding the capital city. For country music's elite, the real estate of choice has always been in one of two areas. You could settle south of Nashville in the Franklin area alongside established superstars like George Jones, Tammy Wynette, and the Judds (plus younger, poppier names like Carrie Underwood and LeAnn Rimes), or you could go north to Hendersonville, where superstars like Johnny Cash built homes on the beautiful Old Hickory Lake, where Roy Orbison had his elegant mansion and Conway Twitty created his own theme park, Twitty City.

Hendersonville is a twenty-minute drive from downtown Nashville and Music Row. Around 40,000 people live there in a community centered on the lake. There's a large shopping mall nearby and pleasant streets occupied by franchise stores and chain restaurants. As you move into the country a little farther, toward the lake area, the roads begin to meander, twist, and wind around the houses as they get grander and are set farther from the road as befits an entertainer/celebrity enclave.

To Scott Swift, buying a decent house by the lake was no problem. It was an ideal location for Swift, combining a peaceful countryside and lake community with a medium-sized city and its internationally connected music industry just a few miles down the road.

At first look the wholesale move, lock, stock, and barrel, from Pennsylvania to Tennessee might appear naïve at best, reckless at worst. Many single adults with no dependents and few family commitments move to Nashville in search of their dreams every day, and the vast majority have a tough time surviving, let alone surfacing above the muddy, choppy waters of the country music business.

But Scott Swift didn't become a successful financial expert by being foolhardy. He was confident that his daughter had the necessary magical and intangible quality to make her successful in entertainment. He had been studying, asking questions, and gathering as much information about her possible path and the potential risks ever since he'd bombarded country singer Pat Garrett with questions back in Pennsylvania.

ATTITUDE IS ALL

The interest of Britney Spears's one-time manager Dan Dymtrow gave Scott Swift confidence that Taylor had an edge, and with Dymtrow arranging for one of Taylor's songs to appear on Maybelline's *Chicks with Attitude* music compilation CD, there was something tangible about the dream. Throw in a show at BMI Songwriter's Circle showcase at the Bitter End in New York, and all the songwriting sessions she'd picked up with decent Nashville songsmiths like Troy Verges and the Warren brothers, plus the low-key but significant development deal with RCA, and Taylor was clearly showing plenty of credit on the Swift family music biz balance sheet.

Taylor was happy to move, and with typical Swift family grace nobody even hinted that the family was putting everything on the line for Taylor's potential talents. As she told pophistorydig.com, "They didn't put me under pressure at all. It wasn't like, 'This is your one shot, so make it happen.' They presented it as a move to a nice community. If I made something out of it, great. But if that didn't happen, that's okay, too." What Swift focused on, as she had learned on her first visit to Nashville as an eleven-year-old, was that songwriting, and more than that, songwriting with others, was going to be the key to her potential success.

Nashville is a co-writing town, and it's rare to see just one name on a songwriter credit on a Nashville album. Some musicians specialize in composing

LEANN RIMES

LEANN Rimes, a prodigiously gifted singer who burst on the country music world in 1996, had a profound effect on the young Taylor Swift. It wasn't just **that she was discovering her love** of country, but also the fact that Rimes, a child little older than Taylor when she hit ig, was a clear signal to overachiever Taylor that her dreams could come true, and fast. As Taylor later said, "My dream idol to meet when I was younger was LeAnn Rimes. It was so cool to see someone who was fourteen years old making albums and touring."

A powerhouse singer as a kid and a regular winner of talent shows in her native Texas, LeAnn Rimes recorded the Patsy Cline–sounding "Blue" when she **was** thirteen, and the song made her a star. Since then she has struggled with all-too-familiar child star issues, moved from country to pop, become a successful international act, and appeared at rock festivals such as Lollapalooza. LeAnn has grown up in public and has never been out of the tabloids, but in the process she has had to learn to deal with downside of life as a celebrity.

After winning most of the local talent shows in Texas available to her, LeAnn Rimes put out an independently released album when she was eleven. Dallas DJ Billy Mack was so impressed with LeAnn's raw talent he came up with a plan to groom the young singer for the top.

Mack had a song, "Blue," that he'd written back in the 1960s. He'd tell the press later that the song was written for Patsy Cline (it certainly sounds perfect for the big-voiced 1960s country diva) but that Cline had died before she was able to record it. Whether or not the legendary Patsy Cline ever heard or considered cutting "Blue" is unclear, but the story made great copy, and when radio stations heard the song and LeAnn's truly powerful vocals, airplay was guaranteed.

The Patsy Cline comparison helped put LeAnn Rimes on the map, and "Blue" was one of the biggest radio hits of 1996, making it to number 10 on the country chart. The following *Blue* album was a monster, too, selling more than 120,000 copies in its first week, the highest number at that point ever recorded by SoundScan. The album sailed to number 1 on the country chart and burst onto the mainstream *Billboard* 200 chart at number 3, selling 4 million copies in the United States and around 8 million internationally.

LeAnn made such an impact on Nashville age fourteen that she was nominated for the Country Music Association Horizon Award. Her crossover success was rewarded when she picked up two Grammys: Best New Artist and Best Female Country Vocal Performance.

Her rise continued with an inspirational album release featuring cover songs that were more pop than country. *Unchained Melody: The Early Years* (1997) was made up of mostly previously recorded songs. Later that year she released "How Do I Live," and it received massive media attention (making number 2 on the *Billboard* Hot 100) when Trisha Yearwood released the same tune at the same time, but recorded in a more country style. Rimes's version was intended for the soundtrack **to** *Con Air* but was considered "too pop," and Yearwood's version was used instead. LeAnn continued to move in a pop direction (she covered Prince's "Purple Rain") with her next album, *Sittin' on Top of the World*, in 1998. The album went platinum, but Rimes was still not convinced about where her music was heading. She returned to the county fold for her next project, *LeAnn Rimes*, which established her as a genuine artist with a slew of great reviews.

As she matured through the 2000s LeAnn developed as a writer, and by the time her album *Family* was released in 2007 she'd had a hand in writing every song on the record. Everyone wanted to ask her about the latest young county singer on the scene, Taylor Swift.

GACTV picked up on some comments she made to Dial-Global Radio Networks: "It's so funny, she [Taylor] used to come to my concerts when she was really little, and of course I was very young too. She would be one of those little girls on the front row that was raising her hands and just wanting to touch me and wanting to sing with me, and it was adorable. So, that's how I remember her—as this tiny little girl coming to my shows." But "be careful out there" was Rimes's message to Taylor; "she's having incredible success and good for her. I just hope that she can keep her feet grounded and not get too far off center."

Rest assured that lifelong LeAnn Rimes fan Taylor Swift, always a quick study, will have noted her childhood favorite LeAnn's words of wisdom.

OPPOSITE: LeAnn Rimes performing at the Grammy Foundation House Concert in 2010.

BELOW: Taylor taking part
in a TV show, *Fox and
Friends*, in New York, 2006.

melodies, others in writing lyrics; there's even rumored to be a song title spe-
cialist in Nashville, on call for those snappy titles that DJs like to talk about on air.
New writers often work in twos and threes, pooling their talents, sharing what tips
they've picked up from other writing sessions. And once writer-artists rise through
the ranks, most also prefer to share the songwriting duties. Country superstar and
Swift favorite Clint Black worked consistently with writing collaborator Hayden
Nicholas, for instance. Alan Jackson has always collaborated with Jim McBride.
Dierks Bentley usually writes with Brett Beavers, while Brad Paisley likes to write
with Kelley Lovelace. Most Nashville songwriters accept that collaboration is the
norm in Music City. Acclaimed songwriter Rodney Crowell explained that "they
set you up with a writer that the publisher thinks will work well with you or complement you and put their writers in a room at ten in the morning and wait for the
songs to come. I personally don't write that way, but I'm an exception in a city that
exists on co-writes."

When the young Garth Brooks first made his mark in Nashville he tried to
write with as many veteran songwriters as he could. "There are so many great
writers in Nashville that it makes sense to work with as many as you can, to learn
from them and have them make your music even better," he reasoned in 1990. Of
course, many well-seasoned veteran writers tuned down Brooks's requests to write,
which was something they would regret for years to come. Indeed, Brooks shook
up the established writing community with the scale of his phenomenal success, so

that since the 1990s, established writers have been far more likely to sit down with a new face than they had been previously. Nobody wants to miss out on the next country music phenomenon.

For a young writer like Taylor Swift, being able to sit down with a seasoned pro, to test her natural instincts with someone who knew the craft of writing songs for radio, was invaluable.

While she had a development deal with RCA, the Swift camp understood that the arrangement was a career boost, but it was a long way from a record deal, and record companies notoriously signed many more artists to development deals than ever graduated to the real world of videos, singles, and albums.

Because so many country singers are not also songwriters they find themselves far more dependent on song publishing companies and record labels to shape their careers. A singer-songwriter is more self-contained, has more to offer, and needs less direction and molding from the so-called Svengalis at the record companies.

MOVING ON

When RCA decided to offer Swift a renewal to her development deal they included a proviso that Swift would be recording songs by other writers. That they didn't have faith in her material was the deciding factor in Swift rejecting the renewal and walking away from RCA Records.

She told *Entertainment Weekly*: "A development deal is where they're giving you recording time and money to record, but not promising that they'll put an album out. And they can kind of shelve you, in some circumstances. After a year of development, we just decided that we wanted to look around, so we walked. And it's not a really popular thing to do in Nashville, to walk away from a major record deal. But that's what I did, because I wanted to find some place that would really put a lot of time and care into this."

Swift's faith in her ability to write songs that matched the sound of country radio in the 2000s was boosted when, after sending her songs to numerous companies in town, Sony ATV, one of the biggest and most prestigious companies in Nashville, showed interest.

Troy Tomlinson, creative director at Sony ATV Tree when Taylor Swift arrived in Nashville, was steeped in country music history. His brother had played bass with Opry star Hank Snow, and Troy had been in the publishing business since he was twenty years old, working his way through the Nashville system. When he heard the young singer's tapes he was immediately impressed. As he told E's *True Hollywood Story*, "What really drew us to her was her songwriting ability. To be able to paint the pictures in three-and-a-half-minute songs that she could was pretty unique for someone of that age."

Typically a songwriter comes to town, finds a nonstressful day job—or, in most cases, a night job working as a waiter in a bar or restaurant—and spends daytime hours treading the streets and trying to write that career-changing song, usually in tandem with other songwriters. For Swift the routine was a little different, as Tomlinson recalls: "Here you had a young lady who would go to high school during the day and as soon as she would finish school, Mom would pick her up and drive her straight down here to our office."

It was Tomlinson's job to assess Taylor Swift's strengths and weaknesses and see how Sony could help develop the goldmine of potential they saw in her. Fortunately, Taylor was unlike most fourteen-year-old girls. She understood that this was a job that needed dedication and hard work. But then Swift was always very driven to succeed. As she told *Songwriter Universe*: "When I signed, I knew that I had to work just as hard as the veteran forty-five-year-old writers who were also signed there. I wrote a lot of songs, which were mainly for my own artist project, rather than writing songs for pitching to other artists."

She also understood that she was a rarity in Nashville, a teenage girl working in an adult world, and she would have to prove herself up to scratch every time she worked with a new and seasoned writer. She told the *New York Times*: "I knew every writer I wrote with was pretty much going to think, 'I'm going to write a song for a 14-year-old today,' so I would come into each meeting with 5 to 10 ideas that were solid. I wanted them to look at me as a person they were writing with, not a little kid." Taylor Swift was confident and composed, and had quickly figured out the benefits of the Nashville co-writing system. In fact, she'd already met the person who would help her grow into a hit songwriter: Liz Rose.

"She was barely fourteen and she had a development deal on RCA," Rose told *American Songwriter* magazine. "RCA had this really cool thing down in their basement they called ROG Café. I went over there and did one of their rounds and it's so funny because I don't sing, but I got up and did a couple of songs, kind of struggled through 'em. I did a song that I wrote with Mark Narmore called 'Nothing Will,' and Taylor came up to me afterwards and introduced herself and told me that she loved the song. 'Would you write sometime?' I said, 'Sure' and we wrote a song called 'Never Mind,' and I remember writing with her and thinking, why am I here? She was so fast and we had fun, and I remember we turned it in and someone said, 'You know, this is really good but do you think you could get her to write something a little more country?' And I said, 'You're not going to get her to do anything she doesn't feel; this kid knows exactly what she's doing.'

"I think she ended up just writing with me because I didn't change what she was doing. I tried to make it better and mold it and hone it, and hang on there and write it down; that's why it worked with us. I really respected and got what she was trying to do and I didn't want to make her write in the Nashville cookie-cutter songwriting mold."

NEVER MIND

Liz Rose had moved to Tennessee from Irving, Texas, in 1994, initially working plugging and pitching other people's songs to music publishers in Nashville. Occasionally she'd co-write with some of the writers she represented. Eventually her talent came to the attention of veteran publishing company owner Jody Williams, who persuaded to her to focus on her songwriting. Swift liked working with Rose; she brought something different to the writing table and took Taylor's work seriously and at face value. "I love writing with Liz," Taylor told *Songwriter Universe*. "When we write, I usually come in with a melody and some lyric content, and then we'll work on creating the rest of the song. She's a really good song editor."

One of the first songs they worked on together was a break-up tune that Swift had been crafting for a while, titled "Tim McGraw." "The song is based on true events—it happened in real life," Swift told *Songwriter Universe*. "I had a boyfriend and we had broken up. After the break-up, I wanted him to be reminded of me. The key lines in the song are: 'When you think Tim McGraw / I hope you think my favorite song / The one we danced to all night long.' There was a specific Tim McGraw song which inspired me—it was 'Can't Tell Me Nothing,' which was on his *Live Like You Were Dying* album."

After Swift and Rose would finish a song it needed to be demoed—that is, recorded to a sufficient quality to present to others. Demos in Nashville are not merely guitar vocal tracks; most songs get the full production treatment, and many times the demo of a song is almost indistinguishable from the released master version.

Nathan Chapman was another young Nashville musician who wanted to be a producer, and when given the opportunity jumped at the chance to produce songwriter demos. It was a way into the Nashville record business and would allow him

to learn the craft and meet the right people. He was getting his own foot in the production door with songs and he was determined to bring something fresh to the Nashville sound. Chapman's willingness to break Nashville formula rules and to try new musical ideas and to be sympathetic to a writer's vision made him a perfect collaborator for Taylor Swift. As he told the *Times Free Press*: "Sometimes you like a song, but that song will wane in appeal over time. It's usually a combination of a gut feeling about a song and how that song appeals the more time passes. My role as producer is to help her get her ideas out. She may have a particular kind of guitar sound in mind; she'll describe it to me, and I'll help her realize that."

ABOVE: **Taylor and Liz Rose at the Grammys, 2010, accepting the award for best country song. Their writing partnership has blossomed since the early days of Taylor's career.**

"My parents moved across the country so I could pursue a dream."

PREVIOUS PAGE: Swift working the crowd during a commercial shoot in 2009.

RIGHT: The Bluebird Cafe in Nashville, where Taylor was able to perform early on in her career, honing her performance skills.

THE BIG MACHINE

Determined to pursue the artist path rather than provide hits for others, Swift played a gig at Nashville's prestigious Bluebird Café to showcase both her vocal and her songwriting talents. The Bluebird is in an unassuming strip mall in Green Hills, a ritzy Nashville suburb that has the most upmarket shopping in Nashville and some of the finest homes in middle Tennessee. It's a hip and fashionable area where the likes of Carrie Underwood and Keith Urban and his wife, Nicole Kidman, are often seen in the local boutiques, health stores, and coffee shops. Across the street from the swanky shopping area, sitting next to a chain gas station, is a small building that would go unnoticed except for certain evenings, when lines of songwriters stretch into the neighboring parking lots with wannabe stars hoping to make the open mike cut, determined to showcase their songs and their talents. It's just a small room inside the café, with tables and some bar seating, but it takes its songwriting very seriously. There's a no-talking rule, strictly enforced when performers take their turn on the tiny stage. This is, as they call it in Nashville, a listening room. Selected writers are given a number, and one after the other they take the stage, thank Nashville for welcoming them, explain their own particular dream and play two or three songs. As writers graduate from these open mike nights, they'll play guest slots with featured acts for evening shows during the week. If a publishing company or record label is confident in an artist they'll arrange a special showcase, an opportunity for the industry movers and shakers to see the new act for themselves.

The Bluebird was opened in 1982, and by the mid-1980s it was the hippest and most significant songwriter venue in Nashville. The wave of new talent that came to town in the wake of the new country movement of the 1980s led to hundreds of young writers knocking at the doors and lining up outside on Sunday and Monday nights to audition for open mike nights. When Garth Brooks, a young writer himself, was signed on the strength of a masterful Bluebird showcase, the venue became all the more prestigious.

On the night Taylor Swift played her own showcase she was seen by one of the brightest and best young record company executives in Nashville, Scott Borchetta, her future record company boss. As she told *Florida Entertainment Scene*: "I had just left a development deal with RCA, so I was doing a showcase for a bunch of different labels. It was just me and my guitar, playing at the Bluebird Cafe in Nashville. Scott Borchetta hadn't even started Big Machine at that time, but he came up to me after the show and said 'I want you to wait for me . . . I'm working on something.' The way he said it convinced me that there was something going on that I probably would want to be a part of."

Scott Borchetta was mulling over his future in the record business when he saw Taylor Swift at the Bluebird. He was one of the coolest, most progressive young music executives in Nashville and had played a vital role in Toby Keith's phenomenal success. Before that he'd been a musician, playing on the road for several country acts before moving to a job with his father's promotions company. His father, Mike Borchetta, was an industry veteran whose career went back as far as working for the Beach Boys in the 1960s. At indie country label Curb in the 1980s, he signed Tim McGraw after one listen to his demo and worked tirelessly on breaking a fourteen-year-old LeAnn Rimes. Later, Borchetta moved to promotions at DreamWorks Records, where he established himself in the radio promotions department working with artists like Randy Travis and Jimmy Wayne.

The next step would be starting his own record label, a company that would be part of the revolution in the way music is delivered and sold, a record label that would understand the new young country demographics better than most in the Music Row community. He told the *Nashville Music Guide* that the business was changing dramatically, thanks to the possibilities and reach of the Internet.

Confident in her own talents and willing to go with her instincts on Scott Borchetta, Swift felt the move to Big Machine Records was the right one. She told the UK's *Daily Mail*, "I knew that he would not try to make me something that I didn't want to be, play some character that I wasn't, fit some mold."

Taylor Swift had the record deal she had dreamed of and worked so hard for. That left only high school to think about.

BELOW: Taylor Swift posing for the press at the 2009 CMAs with Scott Borchetta and Nathan Chapman.

CLINT BLACK

WHEN Taylor Swift first started visiting RCA Records in Nashville, she can't have avoided seeing the impressive Clint Black gold discs displayed around the building. In the 1990s Black, now a respected industry figure, was a prolific songwriter, hit maker, and country music superstar.

It all started for Clint in 1989 with a record deal at RCA. He had spent years honing his singer songwriter craft in Texas. "I played loads of bars and restaurants and to do that you have to know hundreds of songs and be very versatile, while also trying to create your own musical identity as an artist, so that was priceless."

In the early days in Nashville he worked mostly with another songwriter, Hayden Nicholas, and created a style of country that was part traditional country, part West Coast singer-songwriter, and part Texas troubadour. It was a more sophisticated sound than Nashville had been used to. His debut album, *Killin' Time*, was a huge success. His first single, "Better Man," went to number one, the first time a male country artist's debut single had reached the top spot in more than ten years. In all the record gave him five number 1 country singles. The album also topped the charts and went platinum a year later. Clint Black was the sensation at the 1989 CMAs, picking up no less than six awards as well as winning the American Music Awards Favorite New Male Country Artist, Academy of Country Music Best New Male Vocalist, Academy of Country Music Best Male Vocalist, Academy of Country Music Album of the Year (*Killin' Time*), and Academy of Country Music Single of the Year ("A Better Man").

At this time, with a hugely successful music career, Black began dating actress Lisa Hartman of *Knot's Landing* fame. They were married in 1991 and enjoyed a smash hit together with the duet "When I Said I Do" written by Black. The song made it to the Billboard Hot Country Singles # 1 spot in December 1999 and was later nominated for a Grammy. Then things started to stall. First, a dispute over payments with his manager, Bill Ham, led to lawsuits and subsequent delays in putting out new music. Then Black found himself slipping down the country music rankings. The early 1990s were not a good time to sit waiting in the wings. Garth Brooks, who initially lived in Black's shadow, rose to the top at a phenomenal rate. "People forget," says Pam Lewis, who was Brooks's co-manager back then, "Clint Black was huge at the time, way ahead of Garth, and he was major phenomenon."

After that, several new faces sailed into town in Garth's wake, shaking up Nashville with a new energy and style. Both Alan Jackson and Billy Ray Cyrus roared to the top, and country music moved on. Clint Black was still a contender, but his momentum had been lost, and he was unable to re-create the impact of that first record-breaking album.

Aware that he was no longer flavor of the month, Black, always more level-headed than many of his contemporaries, took a sabbatical to spend time with his daughter. He told NPR: "I wanted to be someone that she trusted. And someone that carried her around when she couldn't sleep, and all those things that a lot of dads that don't travel get to do. What a lot of dads don't get to do is tell everybody at the office, 'not today.' I had that luxury, and I took advantage of it. And it wasn't —it didn't complement my career in many ways, but I wouldn't have—I wouldn't go back and try to do anything for my career in exchange for that."

Like many other music stars, Black has also had success with some acting roles. He starting off with a cameo in the 1994 hit movie *Maverick*, starring Jodie Foster and Mel Gibson. Other film roles have included *Still Holding On: The Legend of Cadillac Jack* in 1998 and 2000's *Going Home* (with Jason Robards), and most recently *Flicka 2*. Black has also dabbled in TV, appearing on *The Larry Sanders Show*, *Las Vegas*, and a long run on season two of *Celebrity Apprentice*.

As Taylor Swift's career inevitably levels out from the rocket ride she's experienced so far (as surely it must, one day), Clint Black's smart move in nurturing new talent could very well be a path that Taylor, with her fingers very much on the pulse of her generation, could excel at. In the meantime, she'll doubtless continue to listen to Clint's early albums and enjoy their wit, invention, and catchy hooks.

OPPOSITE: Clint Black performing at halftime of the Super Bowl in 1994.

3

A Perfectly Good Heart

TAYLOR Swift was in her element at Hendersonville High School, just north of Nashville. It was the end of August 2004 and still hot in Tennessee, but a quickly descending cool fall was just around the corner. Away from the narrow minds at her school in Pennsylvania she made a positive new start with kids who had grown up around country music, who were familiar with people pursuing the artistic path in Nashville, and who embraced and supported Taylor's dreams rather than being threatened by them. Taylor told *Elle* magazine: "I had a double life. During the day I walked around, talked to people, went to class, studied for tests, and had crushes on boys, and then after school I would go downtown to Music Row in Nashville and I would write songs about those experiences."

She also found something in Hendersonville she'd been sadly missing in Pennsylvania—a best friend. She met her soon-to-be best friend Abigail Anderson in English class, hitting it off by expressing a shared cynicism about romantic love during a class discussion on *Romeo and Juliet*. Abigail would not only help keep Taylor grounded and introduce her into the Hendersonville social scene, but also provide inspiration for her music, including for her monster hit "Fifteen."

Like most girls her age, Swift was becoming Internet savvy and figured out that she could use social Web site MySpace.com to share her new songs with friends and family. Launching a Taylor Swift MySpace page, she would inadvertently provide the marketing impetus to put her immediately on the map when her music became available commercially. Enjoying writing as much as she did, Taylor also began writing a blog that would provide fascinating insights into her blossoming and accelerating music and showbiz career. Her first blog post in November 2005 shows an excited young singer enthusing about the joys of recording and working toward her dream.

"You only get so many firsts, each one is a blessing."

She told her fans about working with her first producers, Nathan Chapman and Robert Ellis Orrall and Byron Gallimore and she explained to her readers what tracking meant (recording the instrumental parts separately from vocals) and then working on vocals and backing vocals at a later time. Taylor wrote about how excited she was to have done a showcase for some record company executives at Scott Borchettas's house and that her parents had bought her a video camera so she could document everything that was going on. She told how she loved joking around with the band, especially the drummer who kept doing *Napoleon Dynamite* voices. She had discovered that there was usually a lot of down time during long recording sessions when she could be creative and goofy, photocopying her hands with the Intern, for instance. She also told her fans that she loved to work hard, a quality that would be more than valuable the coming months and years.

Initially Big Machine Records and the Swifts did indeed work with several producers before settling on the unknown but open-minded and fresh-sounding young producer Nathan Chapman. "We switched [album] producers a bunch of times," Swift told CMT.com. "I started off with this demo producer who worked

in a little shed behind this publishing company I was at. His name was Nathan Chapman. I'd always go in there and play him some new songs, and the next week he would have this awesome track, on which he played every instrument, and it sounded like a record. We did this for a period of a year to two years before I got my record deal.

"Then, all of a sudden, it was, 'Okay, we're going to use this producer' or 'We're going to use that producer.' So I got to record with a bunch of really awesome producers in Nashville. But it didn't sound the way that it did with Nathan. He had never made an album before. He had just recorded demos. But the right chemistry hit. Finally, my record label president said, 'Okay, try some sides with Nathan.'" In the end, Chapman produced all but one of the cuts.

Since Taylor Swift was fifteen and in her sophomore year at Hendersonville High School when she signed with the fledgling Big Machine Records, music and school had to be carefully scheduled. Borchetta had an unmarked building on Music Row, and every day after school Taylor and her mom would head to the label offices for meetings or to Chapman's recording studio. Her self-titled debut album was recorded in fragmented sessions from June to September 2006 in various Nashville area recording studios, including the Sound Cottage and Quad Studios.

Taylor Swift, remarkably in an industry that prefers to cherry-pick songs for its artists, would write co-write all eleven songs on the album. The first single, "Tim McGraw," was released before the album was finished and would prove to be a significant breakthrough song. Borchetta had the track earmarked for a single ever since Taylor had played it for him in his office a year previously. In many ways it was perfect—a teenage girl's angst-ridden diary entry about an impending break-up, with a clever Tim McGraw twist that would prove priceless as a marketing

BELOW: The home of Big Machine Records in Nashville.

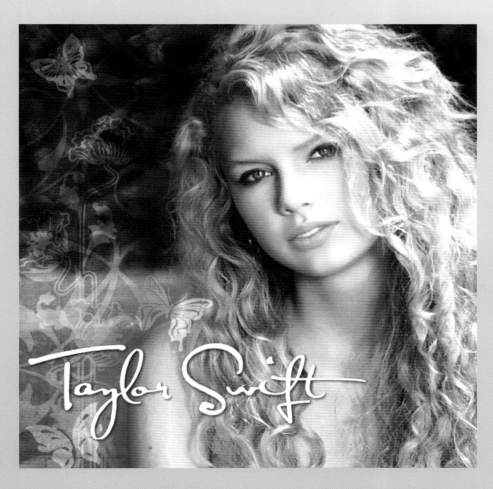

tool. McGraw and his wife, Faith Hill, were huge country stars in 2006 and country music royalty in Nashville, and the name check garnered Swift and Big Machine Records attention that arguably would never have gone their way without the reference.

Taylor Swift told *Musician* magazine: "After I wrote this song, I didn't think it was a hit. I didn't even think it would ever see the light of day. I completely forgot about it, until I was playing my record label president a few songs and my dad said 'Hey, play him that Tim McGraw song you wrote' and with some hesitation (and a 'You're probably going to think this is stupid' warning), I did. He loved it. When I first wrote it, the song was called 'When You Think Tim McGraw,' but whenever we would play it or talk about it, it just got shortened to 'Tim McGraw.'"

With "Tim McGraw," country music was introduced to Taylor Swift's no-holds-barred, honesty-is-the-best-policy approach to songwriting. More than most in pop music, her autobiographical songs were practically all direct accounts of real life events. With Big Machine Records still in start-up mode, the first single's release was very much a family affair. She told E's *True Hollywood Story*: "My whole family and my co-writers and my producer all sat in the tiny lobby of the building and we put singles in envelopes."

Another song on the album, "The Outside," was written when Taylor was twelve years old and dealing with rejection in Pennsylvania. It was the start of Swift using music to help deal with the pains of adolescence and the loneliness she was dealing with as she became a teenager. She told CMT.com: "I was going through a really tough time in school and facing a lot of rejection among my peers. I found that I was alone a lot of the time, kind of on the outside looking into their discussions and the things they were saying to each other. They really didn't talk to me. In the process of coming to that realization, I started developing this really keen sense of observation, of how to watch people and see what they did. From that sense, I was able to write songs about relationships when I was 13 but not in relationships."

"Tied Together with a Smile" arose from her discovering that a friend was suffering from the eating disorder bulimia; "Mary's Song (Oh My My My)" was inspired by her neighbors' long-lasting marriage, while, in typical Swift fashion, "Our Song" was written quickly because she and the boy she was dating didn't have their own song. "Invisible" is a page from Swift's diary, an account of feeling ignored and insignificant. Swift apparently came up with "Should've Said No" as a last-minute song, added just as the album was being put to bed. "Basically, it's about a guy who cheated on me and shouldn't have because I write songs," she told CMT.com.

With DJs curious about the song title and Tim McGraw fans clamoring to hear it, the success of "TimMcGraw" was almost inevitable. It eventually reached as high as number 6 on the *Billboard* country chart, although it took some time to get there. The album followed the single's success, helping it to sell 39,000 copies in its first week of release. The album quickly reached the top spot of the *Billboard* album chart, staying there for more than twenty of ninety one weeks—putting Taylor in the exceptional company of Carrie Underwood and the Dixie Chicks in taking the number 1 slot for twenty weeks or more in the 2000s. It was a remarkable feat for a new artist at a time of economic slowdown, and particularly with drastic changes in the record business that had hurt country music sales in general.

"Teardrops on My Guitar," a stronger song perhaps than "Tim McGraw" in many ways, consolidated Swift as more than a teenage one-hit wonder. Released in February 2007, the song reached the number two slot on the *Billboard* chart and demonstrated Swift's immediate crossover potential, rising to number thirty–three on the *Billboard* pop chart. A later pop remix of the single pushed the song as high as number thirteen on the Hot 100 chart.

GET OUT THERE AND SING!

While country music is changing some of its previously entrenched ideas and business practices, country artists still tour far more than their pop counterparts. It's part of what makes the country music machine work, and Nashville is geared to get new acts on the road as soon as possible to support radio play and set up nationwide meet-and-greet situations that will benefit the artist enormously down the road. Big Machine Records set up an extensive radio tour that involved Taylor showing up at many of the more than 2,500 country music radio stations in the United States to play a song or two on air or conduct an short interview and meet the radio community who had her success in their hands. She told CMT.com: "Radio tours for most artists last six weeks. Mine lasted six months. That's because I wanted it to. I wanted to meet every single one of the people that was helping me out."

Shannon McCombs has been one of Nashville's premier radio and TV personalities for the past twenty years, interviewing everyone from Garth Brooks to Rod Stewart and Jay Leno. From the start, she recalls, Taylor Swift won over the country media with charm and an infectious personality. "I've interviewed Taylor several times and her approach to me has always been the same. Always friendly, always professional and always tries to put *you* and everyone else in the room at ease. She's a good interview, too. Some artists just waste your time with their rambling answers, but not Taylor. She knows this is her career and she pays attention to details. She has no fear of walking up to you first to say hello. Another thing I've noticed working with her, if she walks into the studio or my interview room and doesn't know everyone, and everyone isn't introduced to her . . . she will introduce herself."

Aside from radio tours, Taylor Swift needed to be playing live, and slowly but surely Big Machine introduced their new starlet to the world via opening slots with some of the biggest names in country music, starting with pop-country

OPPOSITE: Taylor arriving at the Academy of Country Music Awards in Las Vegas, in 2007.

superstars Rascal Flatts. Taylor blogged on October 17, 2006 about being asked to open some shows for one of country's hippest, most popular young acts, Rascal Flats. Unfortunately this meant postponing some previously booked concerts in Pennsylvania but Taylor took the time to announce this change and apologize for the inconvenience on her MySpace page as well as telling her fans that she'd be back in PA as soon as she could. She also blogged excitedly a few days before the release of her album about the coded secret messages embedded in the lyrics booklet that was going to come with the albums. "Look for the random capitalized letters," she said, and you would see the hidden messages about her songs.

Confident beyond her years, an excited Swift leaped at the chance to open for Rascal Flatts and perform five songs, "Play It Again," "Teardrops on My Guitar," "Should've Said No," "Tim McGraw," and "Picture to Burn."

Swift seized the opportunity with typically accomplished performances. Bobbi Smith at About.com was "very impressed with her stage presence and her ability to interact with the audience so easily. A lot of times newer, and especially younger, acts haven't learned how to connect with the audience and they seem nervous, or distant. But Taylor exhibited none of that. She talked between songs and took command of the stage with ease."

"I never want to change so much that people can't recognize me."

During the concerts, before singing "Teardrops on My Guitar," Swift would use a spoken intro, which would become a trademark in her burgeoning career. She said, "I always try to be nice . . . but if you break my heart, you cheat on me, or you're really mean to me . . . I'll write a song about you." It was something a few unknown and some very well-known figures would discover to be true in the months ahead.

After proving to be a success on the Rascal Flatts dates, her next move was to open for one of country music's most legendary established stars, George Strait. The Rascal Flatts audience is much younger, a more obvious fit for a teenage girl singer than Strait's older, more traditional demographic. If Swift's mix of country, pop, and from-the-heart lyrics could win over Strait fans, then she really was a bona fide country music artist. It was announced that she would join George Strait's arena tour coming up in January 2007. Swift was excited and honored, telling CMT News, "I couldn't imagine anything more thrilling than to be on a tour with George Strait," Swift said. "Just last week, I was at the CMA Awards watching him be inducted into the Hall of Fame, and this week I received word that I would be on the tour with him. This is surreal! I keep pinching myself to make sure this isn't just a dream."

With Taylor Swift's country star rising rapidly she was added to Brad Paisley's tour alongside Jack Ingram and Kellie Pickler, which criss-crossed America starting in April 2007. That summer, the girl who kicked it all off with the song "Tim McGraw" performed on select dates on Tim McGraw and Faith Hill's Soul2Soul tour.

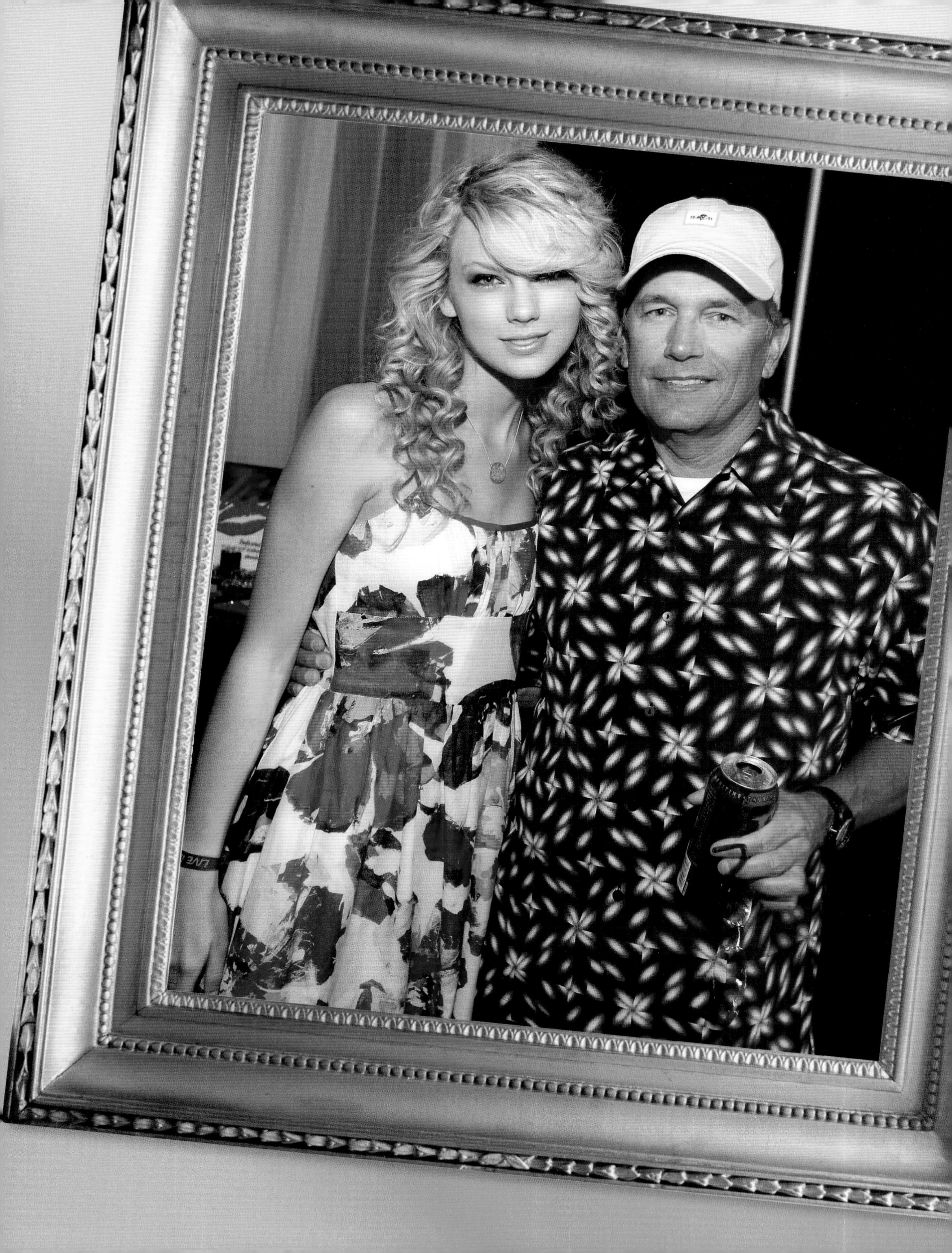

Swift had actually met Tim McGraw for the first time when she performed at the Academy of Country Music Awards in Las Vegas. She didn't win that year, but she picked up the Breakthrough Video of the Year award for "Tim McGraw" at the fan-voted CMT Awards in Nashville. She wrote on her MySpace blog that she couldn't really believe what was happening to her. She'd always been the girl watching awards shows from the stands on her couch just wishing that if she worked hard enough she might be the one receiving an award one day. She wanted the fans to know how grateful she was and that she had absolutely enjoyed the thrill of receiving a CMT Award. With the all-important radio community falling for the Swift charm and concertgoers impressed enough with her opening slots to seek out her album, Taylor Swift went platinum (one million sales) in June 2007. There was another factor at play too—Taylor's voracious use of social media.

TO ALL MY FRIENDS

By mid-July 2007, Taylor Swift was easily the top country artist on MySpace.com, with more than 20 million streams, ahead of mega-pop names like Justin Timberlake and 50 Cent. She also reached the phenomenal number of 360,000 MySpace friends. A new Taylor Swift fan site collective—known as the Taylor Nation—was set up and would grow exponentially on the Web. Taylor Swift instinctively understood the demographic she was playing for, and that social media wasn't just a marketing tool, it was a key part of her and their lives. She told the *Modesto Bee*: "I think MySpace has worked so well because I didn't want to make it like every other artist's page, with a third-person bio that was completely not personal," she said. "Instead of doing that, I wrote a first-person bio about what I like and dislike. It is about what I am as a person, not my accomplishments. It lets them in and lets them know it's me running it, not a company. I love the fact that people my age are paying attention to my music. I know how my friends and I look at music and address music—either they love something or don't like it at all."

Significantly, Taylor's crossover appeal to both country and pop audiences was already setting her up for an international career, something country hadn't seen since Garth and Shania in their heyday. The album hit the number fourteen spot on the Canadian album chart and the top spot on the Canadian country chart. Australia followed suit with Swift at number thirty–three on the pop chart and number three on the country chart. Success in the UK, ever since the Beatles revolutionized pop music in the 1960s, has held great sway with American record labels, but few in Nashville have pulled it off. However, the signs were more than promising when Taylor Swift entered the UK pop chart at number eighty–eight.

Taylor Swift, unusually for someone as young and with such a pop sound, was winning over the Nashville establishment, which typically preferred more traditional-sounding country music. Her peers in the industry recognized the same kind of work ethic and determination to succeed that colored Garth Brooks's early years. Music Row respected Taylor and her family for their dedication. Shannon McCombs explains it this way: "She also paid a lot of dues before her label deal. She and her family worked hard and spent a lot of time in Nashville making it happen . . . by that she gained a lot of respect in the industry."

In October 2007, Swift became the youngest ever recipient of the prestigious Nashville Songwriters Association International (NSAI) Songwriter/Artist of the Year Award, tied with Alan Jackson.

The third single from the debut album, "Our Song," was number one on the country chart and rose as high as number sixteen on the pop chart. Taylor Swift, incredibly for a new artist, struck a deal with Target stores for an exclusive Christmas album, *Sounds of the Season: The Taylor Swift Holiday Collection*, which was released in time for the holiday season of 2007.

"I wish all teenagers can filter through songs instead of turning to drugs and alcohol."

With her debut album at the top of the country charts, Taylor Swift would end a phenomenal year with the biggest prize so far. The Country Music Association Awards, known as the CMAs, are the Oscars of country music. CMT Awards and Academy of Country Awards are nice, but a CMA is the industry standard, with insiders and peers voting on the yearly achievements of Nashville's finest. Taylor Swift was nominated for the CMA's new artist category, the Horizon Award. Not only is the award prestigious, but the ceremony is televised live on the ABC network for a worldwide audience. On November 8, 2007, Carrie Underwood, the reigning queen of country crossover, presented Swift with a CMA Horizon Award. Taylor later blogged that when Carrie Underwood made the announcement the moment went into slow motion and she recalled running up stairs in a long dress and heels while her parents were crying.

Her acceptance speech was pure Taylor, humble, appreciative, and witty. "I can't even believe this is real. I want to thank God and my family for moving to Nashville so that I could do this, and I want to thank country radio. I will never forget the chance you took on me. Brad Paisley, thank you for letting me tour with you. Scott Borchetta, everybody at Big Machine Records, and the fans: You have changed my life. I can't even believe this. This is definitely the highlight of my senior year!"

The year could hardly get better, but in Taylor's case it did. The CMAs are country music's most prestigious industry awards, but they pale in comparison to the Grammys. In December 2007, Taylor Swift received her first Grammy nomination for Best New Artist, a truly remarkable achievement for any new artist, let alone one still to turn 18. Could 2008 possibly live up to the events of 2007?

BELOW: Taylor thrills the crowd, performing at the 2007 Country Music Awards in Nashville.

FAITH HILL

THE funny thing about the music business is that success can turn heroes into pals. Taylor Swift, who idolized Faith Hill as a kid, ended up staying in Faith and hubby Tim McGraw's Hollywood house while she was in LA shooting her *CSI* episode. She'd become friends with Faith and Tim after joining them on the Soul2Soul II tour, but Taylor's admiration for Faith went back as far as she could remember. So finally meeting Hill was a heart-stopping moment in Taylor's life. She told *ForUs* magazine: "I was always so nervous to meet her and when I finally did at the ACMs in 2007, she was the sweetest celebrity I'd ever met." And when she went on the road with Nashville's favorite married couple, Taylor recalled that Faith "would always leave presents in my dressing room."

Faith Hill, one of country's biggest ever female stars, has plenty of kind words for Taylor Swift, too: "She's in the moment. And that's a lesson for all of us. She's soaking it all in and she's experiencing some great, great things in her life and career. She's a great girl. I like her a lot."

Faith Hill was one of the biggest crossover acts of the 1990s, selling more than 40 million albums worldwide with eight U.S. number one singles. Her last three album releases, 1999's *Breathe*, 2002's *Cry*, and 2005's *Fireflies*, all debuted consecutively at number one on *Billboard*'s top pop album chart and country chart, making her the only female artist ever to accomplish this feat.

Her and Tim McGraw's 2006 Soul2Soul II tour (which Taylor joined for part of the way the following year) became the highest-grossing country live show of all time. No wonder *Billboard* named Hill the number 1 adult contemporary artist of the decade for 2000–2009.

If anyone was destined for superstardom it was Faith Hill from the appropriately named Star, Mississippi. She moved to Nashville when she was nineteen, determined to make it as a singer. She tried out as a backup singer for Reba McEntire but failed the audition—just before many of Reba's band were killed in a plane crash in California in 1991. She found work in Nashville, however, and sang around town at night. She told TV's Larry King about her big break: "I was singing with a songwriter named Gary Burr. I was singing backgrounds

for him. I worked on my background singing. And Martha Sharp, an executive from Warner Brother Records, happened to be in the audience that night and she **came** up to me afterwards and asked if I wanted to . . . if I wanted to make a record, if that's what I was striving to do, what my ambitions were. Did I have a tape?"

Her debut album, *Take Me as I Am*, was a hit mainly thanks to the snappy first single taken from it, "Wild One." It put her on the map as the hip young singer with movie star looks that Nashville had been waiting for. She was engaged to record company boss Scott Hendricks when she embarked on the Spontaneous Combustion tour with Tim McGraw in 1996. There was romance and scandal to follow as she broke off her engagement and fell passionately in love with the handsome country singer then riding high with his smash hit "I Like It, I Love It."

They married in October 1996, eventually had three daughters together, and have never spent more than four consecutive nights away from each other since. So much for scandal!

After a family break, Faith returned to the music scene in 1998 with a more mainstream pop sound on *Faith*. The single "This Kiss" was her first to make the pop charts followed by the sublime "Breathe," which topped every chart there was.

Faith's try for a movie career stalled with the panned *Stepford Wives*, but she bounced back from the disappointment with a back-to-basics country album that Nashville loved and embraced, *Fireflies*, in 2005. In 2007 she did something very cool when she became the voice of the National Football League on Sunday Night Football. Now a close friend to Taylor, she and McGraw are still an inspiration and role models for the young star.

Faith was the golden girl of country music when Taylor was learning her craft, and she showed that, if done gracefully and with courtesy to both music genres, it's very possible to enjoy successful careers in both pop and country music. Faith Hill has also managed to combine her career with raising kids, which is surely something the ever observant Swift has noticed when hanging out with Faith and Tim in Los Angeles.

OPPOSITE: Taylor with her idol and now her friend and supporter, Faith Hill.

4
Beautiful Eyes

TAYLOR launched herself into a series of magazine cover shoots and even more concerts, and in April she really made her mark in popular culture when *People* magazine put her on their Most Beautiful People list. She picked up another couple of honors at the CMT Awards in April, and her MySpace page zoomed ever closer to the crazy fifty million video stream mark.

The more shows Taylor played, the more natural and easy she became with an audience. By spring, when the Academy of Country Music Awards came around she had developed into an accomplished stage performer, ready perhaps to compete with the likes of Miley Cyrus and Lady Gaga on the world stage.

Picking up the ACM's Top New Female Vocalist award was rewarding, but her dramatic live performance of "Should've Said No" proved to be career changing. A typically cozy country music style beginning to the song began with a hooded Swift strumming gently to the camera before it gave way to musical theater theatrics. Swift threw her guitar aside and two dancers appeared to remove her hoodie, revealing a black dress. For the high-energy song's climax Taylor slid to the rear of the stage and performed under falling rain. It was dramatic, unexpected, and radical for a country music show. She received a standing ovation and proved that she really was ready to take on the best.

Taylor Swift, thanks to the speed and unexpected scale of commercial success, now faced something of a dilemma after the release of her debut album. Sales for a new artist had far exceeded expectations despite launching during a period of economic recession for both the U.S. economy and the record business.

By June 2008, *Taylor Swift* was officially triple platinum album, having sold three million units, and had been received well by radio and the media in both country music and pop. But Team Taylor knew she'd really be judged on the all-important second album. The first might have been a lucky break, selling on the strength of a couple of snappy tunes from a young, almost novelty singer. Although country music wasn't known for its one-hit wonders, pop music was, and Taylor was straddling both camps. The follow-up release, on which Swift intended to showcase her own music again, would have to be as good as or even better than the overachieving debut album.

PREVIOUS PAGE: Filming at the CMA Music Festival, 2008.

OPPOSITE AND BELOW: Taylor's dramatic performance of "Should've Said No" during the Academy of Country Music Awards in 2008, which began slowly before ending under falling rain.

I HEART?

Time constraints on a successful new artist are very demanding. The whirl-wind of success, new commitments, business deals, and record promotion tasks typically come as a shock to new acts who are unprepared for the nonmusic side of the artist life. When a new artist is also responsible for all the new songs, the pressure becomes more intense. Taylor Swift would also be writing all the songs for the second album. She needed time to get every task accomplished as well as she could and deliver an album that fans and critics would respect.

In the meantime, such was her success and growing fan base that new music was demanded by her new followers. And with Swift sitting in the center of the social media hurricane and very much in tune with her audience, she and Big Machine knew that the fans had to be given something.

That something was *Beautiful Eyes*, an EP, or mini album. Taylor told country music cable channel GAC: "I thought this might tide them over till the new album comes out in the fall."

In June 2008 Taylor Swift had announced a lucrative marketing arrangement with the vast superstore chain Walmart to represent L.e.i. jeans. Part of the deal included the right to release a CD/DVD exclusive to Walmart.

On July 15, Big Machine released *Beautiful Eyes*, containing six tracks of new material and different versions of songs from her debut album as well as a DVD with rare and previously unseen footage. The DVD was the selling point for many fans, since it included the official music videos as well as fan-oriented backstage features and a Taylor interview.

Concerned that fans might confuse this release with a new album, Taylor quickly blogged on her MySpace page on July 7 to explain that the new album, *Beautiful Eyes*, was not the one she'd been working on all year but it was a limited-edition CD and DVD package. The CD, she said, had unreleased songs "Beautiful Eyes"

OPPOSITE: Taylor at the MTV Studios, 2008.

RIGHT: The first album, which had sold three million copies by 2008.

and "I heart?" as well as different versions of "Should've Said No," and "Teardrops on My Guitar." The DVD, she explained, would feature the "Beautiful Eyes" music video as well as exclusive footage from her eighteenth birthday party. She stressed that *Beautiful Eyes* had a limited run and that she hoped the new material would please the fans who had been e-mailing her, asking for new songs, and tide them over till the fall when the new album would be ready.

The mini album was available exclusively through U.S. Walmart stores, so was available only to American fans. The record sold almost as well as her debut album. In its first week of release, the EP sold 45,000 copies, debuting at number 1 on *Billboard*'s Top Country Albums and number nine on the *Billboard* 200 albums chart. It would stay on the *Billboard* 200 for twenty weeks in total. In the country music world, naturally, the album did even better than Big Machine had anticipated. *Beautiful Eyes* debuted at number one on the Top Country Albums chart, knocking a certain Taylor Swift off the top spot, making Taylor the first country artist to be number one and number two on the country album chart since LeAnn Rimes had achieved the same feat in 1997.

Amid all the entertainment world craziness, Swift was still a schoolgirl, albeit one with a 4.0 GPA and straight A's. She'd quit Hendersonville High for home schooling in an attempt to free up her crammed schedule. High school had been fine and a wonderful place for Taylor to grow to maturity (and find material for her music), but with record industry commitments increasing by the day, the only sensible option was Aaron Academy, a private school specializing in home schooling. The toughest part would be leaving her confidante Abigail behind. It wasn't easy on either friend as Abigail Anderson recalled to the 49News channel in Topeka, Kansas: "I mean, any girl knows that if your best friend leaves you in tenth grade, it's just like, 'Okay, what do I do now?' So, it was hard for both of us," Anderson said. "I had to kind of make a new name for myself around school, and she had to do her own thing out there and miss everything that had been her life for the previous few years. But she just immediately just started doing so well . . . you just couldn't really think about anything else."

Swift, an all-round high achiever as her meteoric country music career might suggest, tackled home schooling with relish and ease. In July 2008 she received her high school diploma in the mail. "Education has always been at the forefront of my priorities, so I'm really glad to have my diploma," she told the Associated Press. And if that wasn't enough, she was about to collaborate with one of the biggest rock bands in history. They were a band of UK rockers who Taylor knew plenty about, since her mother was a huge fan when Taylor was an infant: Def Leppard.

"My mom was a huge fan of theirs when she was pregnant with me," Swift told *People* magazine. "So growing up, the music that was playing in my house was Def Leppard. It was music that she liked that I could like too."

CROSSROADS

CMT's popular series *Crossroads* teamed country artists with rock acts, like Lindsey Buckingham with Little Big Town, Bon Jovi with Sugarland, and Robert Plant with Alison Krauss. Once Swift conceived of the idea doing the show with her mom's favorite Brit rockers, fate intervened. While on tour with Tom McGraw and Faith Hill she found out that their tour manager was none other than the brother of Def Leppard drummer Rick Allen.

"I went on tour with Tim [McGraw] and Faith [Hill]," Swift told *Channel Guide Magazine*, and I found out through the grapevine that Tim and Faith's tour manager was [Def Leppard drummer] Rick Allen's brother . . . So I started totally geeking out . . . I walked up to Robert Allen, the tour manager, and said, 'Is there any way that I could have your brother's number?' And he said, 'Um, no. But I could maybe arrange a phone call.' I get on the phone, and it's this guy with a

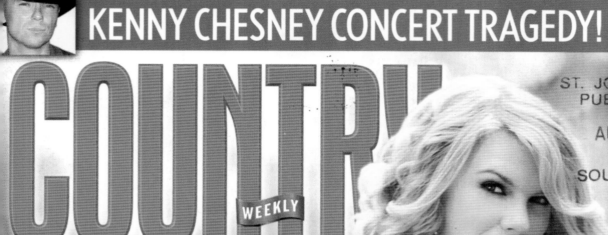

COUNTRY
WEEKLY

THE WORLD'S #1 SELLING COUNTRY ENTERTAINMENT MAGAZINE
SEPTEMBER 8, 2008

George Strait &
George Strait Jr.

STAR KIDS
THEN & NOW

50¢ LESS than People Country

TAYLOR SWIFT
LESSONS I'VE LEARNED

EXCLUSIVE INTERVIEW AND PHOTOS

The young star on:
Family & Friends
Falling in love
Being a role model

BLAKE SHELTON
Wants To Take You "Home"

BROOKS & DUNN
In Trouble With Their Wives?

PLUS
**Trace Adkins
Sara Evans
Randy Travis
Gretchen Wilson
& Many More**

VOTE INSIDE!
COUNTRY'S BEAUTIFUL WOMEN

www.countryweekly.com

ALAN JACKSON
50 MILLION REASONS TO SMILE

British accent named Rick Allen. I was like, 'Hi, you don't know who I am at all. You don't know me or my music, probably, but I'm a new country artist, my name is Taylor and there's this thing on CMT, which is Country Music Television, where they pair up rock acts with country acts and it's a concert called Crossroads. My dream Crossroads partner is you guys, and I would really like it if you would do that with me—could you do that with me?' And he was probably thinking, 'Who is this kid?' And I said, 'So, do you think that you could think about that?' and he was like, 'Well, uh, maybe I could ask the guys about it. Good talking to you.' So, I basically threw it out there that I really wanted to do a Crossroads with them, and then I didn't hear anything for, like, six months. I was like, 'Eh, yeah, that probably didn't work. I probably freaked him out, like, in stalker mode.'

"I got a call from my record label like maybe six or seven months after that phone call, and they said, 'Def Leppard just called. You're on their radar, they know who you are, they've heard your music and they're interested in the Crossroads.' And I was really excited about it."

OPPOSITE: A dream come true as Taylor performs the national anthem before a game between the Tampa Bay Rays and the Philadelphia Phillies in 2008.

"I'm not opposed to falling in love."

As for Def Leppard, Joe Elliott explained that he and the band were barely aware of Taylor Swift when she brought up the CMT show idea. "It was simply a case of somebody forwarding us an interview that she did on some Internet site. It just got brought up with her, that she said, 'I'd love to [do] a *Crossroads*, but there's only one band I would ever do it with, and it's Def Leppard. I love those guys.' Somebody forwarded it to us and we read it and were like, 'Who the hell is Taylor Swift?' because we've been trapped in our little cocoon, not listening to CMT or country music channels very often—not really sure who she was. And then we learned—'What do you mean her first album sold three million copies already?' It's like, 'Wow, you've got to be kidding me.' So we just basically said, 'Why don't we get in touch with her and see if she wants to do it?' So we did, and she very kindly said, 'Yeah, cool.'"

"The Taylor Swift thing should be really interesting," guitarist Vivian Campbell told the *Tennessean* newspaper. "She's only eighteen, but a big Leppard fan. I have really no idea how it's going to work. We're not a very subtle band. I always say our dynamic range is between nine and a half and ten. We're not the best at toning it down."

The pairing with rock legends would be a great boost for new artist Taylor Swift, but would it make sense or even be appealing for veteran rockers who'd been round the rock-and-roll block more than a few times already?

Then again, Swift's huge album sales and valuable young demographic could hardly harm their profile. Moreover, her brand of slick country pop was not so far removed from the softer side of Leppard. Their country roots after all dated back to their days with producer Mutt Lange, the husband of country queen Shania Twain. Def Leppard guitarist Phil Collen explained the connection to

Gibson.com: "Mutt was a huge country fan, as anybody who hung around with him back when he was working with us and AC/DC would tell you. There would always be George Jones and Hank Williams cassettes sliding around the seats of his car."

"I think what's happened is that country music has evolved to embrace the kind of pop and rock that's always been our mainstay," said Collen. "So our guitar sound is now something Nashville's caught up with."

And so, on October 6, Taylor Swift and Def Leppard climbed on stage at the famed Roy Acuff Theater in Nashville in front of a standing-room-only audience to mix country and rock. An enthusiastic Joe Elliott and a barely containable Taylor Swift belted out the hits, notably "Photograph," "Hysteria," "Pour Some Sugar on Me," "Picture to Burn," and "Love Story."

"Performing with Def Leppard was awesome!" said Swift. "It was the coolest thing in the world to have my band on stage with them, because for the past two years, before we go on stage we listen to Def Leppard and just rock out and jump around. And then, we were playing on the same stage as they were. It was the most amazing feeling in the world, and we were all just trying to act cool the whole time."

"What an absolute pleasure it was to work with Taylor and her band who are a great set of musicians," said Def Leppard frontman Joe Elliott. "Myself and Taylor blended really well together, I think, and everybody, both bands and the crowd, had a great time. I'm really glad we had the opportunity to do this.

"A lot of her songwriting's very similar to what we were doing on like, the *Hysteria* and the *Adrenalize* albums, so it was easy to do," Elliott said. "But the performance was just a blast. It just all fell into place, it was fantastic. She got to sing some of our stuff, I got to sing some of hers. And, it just took us out of our normal day-to-day routine, and that was the appeal as much as anything, was the fact that, we were flattered that somebody that was so popular wanted to work with us, but it was the fact that it was also different as well . . . it just made, it just added extra spark to what we normally do."

Mind you, enjoyable as it was, Def Leppard harbored no plans to "go country." Elliott told the Web site www.theboot.com: "That would be untrue to ourselves. But if somebody came in with a song that was slightly leaning toward country, and we thought it was the right thing to do, I don't see why not. It's a very fine line now . . . a lot of the country acts sound like rock bands now."

Def Leppard's dynamic performance with Taylor Swift became the first of CMT's *Crossroads* programs to be released as a DVD, exclusively through Walmart.

PICTURE TO BURN

In October, Taylor Swift received notice that she'd been nominated for an American Music Award (AMA). Typically she expressed her excitement at the nomination on her MySpace page. She wanted all of the fans to know much she appreciated them and that since the American Music Awards were fan-voted she urged them to log on and help her win, as if she needed to ask. That same month, she was honored to be asked to sing the National Anthem at a World Series baseball game, featuring the Tampa Bay Rays against—who else—the Philadelphia Phillies.

On November 8, 2008, Taylor sat down to watch the CMT broadcast of her performance with Def Leppard. She did not relax for long, though. There were CMA Awards show dresses to organize and travel plans to make for the American Music Awards in L.A., where she'd been nominated for the first time. Oh, and there was something else: the eagerly anticipated release of her new album, *Fearless*, a record destined to make Taylor Swift a worldwide superstar and bring not a little personal and professional drama into her so-far fairytale life.

DEF LEPPARD

**A**FTER collaborating with Taylor on an edition of *CMT Crossroads*, Def Leppard singer Joe Elliot said, "She's a great girl to work with. She's so enthusiastic, because she's so young and talented. Everything's going for her right now."

Def Leppard, one of the mega stadium bands of the 1980s and best known for radio smash and arena hit "Pour Some Sugar on Me," started out in the old steel town of Sheffield in northern England. They were poor, their city was dying economically, and music seemed like their only way out.

Rick Savage is the only remaining member of the band's original incarnation, then named Atomic Mass, which featured Pete Willis on bass and Tony Kening on drums. A young Joe Elliott wanted to play guitar with them, but he could sing so well that he became their vocalist. It was Elliott who named the band Def Leppard (intentionally misspelled).

In 1978, a couple of years into England's punk explosion, Steve Clark, ignoring the minimalist guitar playing that was in vogue, auditioned for the band with his version of Lynyrd Skynyrd's southern rock standard "Free Bird" and was given the job instantly. Their drummer left just as they were to record their first tracks, and they found a sub for the sessions; however, the permanent job soon went to a fifteen-year-old kid named Rick Allen.

BBC Radio One DJ John Peel (not a man known for his championing of good old-fashioned rock music at the time) fell in love with the kids from Sheffield and showcased their recently recorded "Getcha Rocks Off" on his ultra cool and hugely influential night-time radio show. Subsequently, Def Leppard got themselves a major record deal.

Nothing too much happened for the band until iconic rock producer Mutt Lange joined the story in 1981. Fresh from working with Australian hard rockers AC/DC and the more pop sounding Boomtown Rats, Lange recognized Def Leppard's talent and potential for hits and produced *High 'n' Dry* for them. Although the album didn't set the world alight, the puzzle pieces were almost all there. Their next album would make them, and Lange worked his magic in typically meticulous but inspired fashion. When *Pyromania* appeared in 1983, containing the smash single "Photograph," Def Leppard had made it to the big time. They soon became a genuine, stadium-filling rock-and-roll band. But then, as happens so often in rock and roll, things started to fall apart.

Personal issues drove a wedge between band members. Mutt Lange was no longer involved on new recording sessions—which just weren't working. Then disaster struck as drummer Rick Allen lost an arm in a car accident on New Year's Eve 1984. Gloriously, the men's friendships proved stronger than band egos and Def Leppard rallied around Allen, possibly to the detriment of their career. They simply would not countenance replacing their buddy. Fortunately Allen, with some technical help, found a way to play again. Mutt returned and the band released the hit-laden *Hysteria* in 1987. It sold twenty million copies.

The band took another blow when Steve Clark died of an overdose in 1991. They chose to continue despite the tragic loss, and the next album, *Adrenalize*, topped both the U.S. *Billboard* 200 and the UK Album Chart in 1992 and delivered more arena hits, including "Let's Get Rocked" and "Have You Ever Needed Someone So Bad."

In 1992 former Whitesnake and Dio guitarist Vivian Campbell joined Def Leppard, but with musical fashion changing fast in the grungy 1990s, the band appeared to be a little off the rock-and-roll pace. It proved to be a tough decade for them, as Campbell told the *Tennessean* newspaper in 2008: "I guess any band from the '80s had a hard time in the '90s getting any kind of respect. But we kept going ahead and making new music, and so many bands of the genre gave up and broke up and we never did."

The Sheffield rockers were made of tough stuff and survived pretty much anything that was thrown at them, and have now achieved iconic status with more than sixty-five million albums sold. They were always a huge live draw and hit the road again in 2011.

OPPOSITE: Frontman with Def Leppard, Joe Elliot, performing onstage.

5

Fearless

SCOTT Borchetta answered his phone. It was Taylor, calling on the eve of her album being finished and then sent out to reviewers. She wanted to add a brand new song, a break-up song that was fresh and painful.

Borchetta told her on E's *True Hollywood Story*, "Here's the deal. We have to go in, cut the track, you have to sing it, and we have to send it out the next day." Taylor agreed, and Nathan Chapman remembers, "We recorded it in the morning and she approved the mix that evening from New York City."

With Swift at the top of her game and putting the finishing touches to her all–important second album in the late summer of 2008, she had embarked on an intense relationship with a fellow music star, Joe Jonas of the teen heartthrob group, The Jonas Brothers.

She'd made a cameo appearance in the boys' 3D movie and had been seen around town with Joe, shifting the celebrity columnists into overdrive. In August, *People* magazine ran a headline that said: "Joe Jonas and Taylor Swift: New Couple?"

When pushed, Taylor simply said, "He's an amazing guy and anybody would be lucky to be dating him." Joe Jonas was similarly coy when radio and TV host Ryan Seacrest asked about the Swift rumors: "She's a great girl . . . I think anybody would love to go on a date with her."

"You need to be happy with yourself or you'll never be able to be happy in a relationship."

The rumors turned out to be true, and while the couple kept their affair very quiet and under the tabloid radar, it all came out when Taylor talked about their sudden and painful breakup on the *Ellen* show. "You know what it's like, when I find that person that is right for me, he'll be wonderful . . . When I look at that person, I'm not even going to remember the boy who broke up with me over the phone in twenty-five seconds when I was eighteen . . . I looked at the call log—it was like twenty-seven seconds. That's got to be a record."

The song Taylor had wanted added to *Fearless* at the last minute was "Forever and Always," a song version of her short-lived romance and split with Joe Jonas. "[It's] a song about watching somebody completely fade away in a relationship and wondering what you did wrong," she told *People* magazine.

But, once scorned, Taylor Swift wasn't afraid to tell the world her side of the story. Suitors beware. As she told Britain's *Daily Mail*, "If guys don't want me to write songs about them, they shouldn't do bad things! And if they're afraid, going into the relationship, that they're going to end up having a bad song written about them . . . Well, then they don't have the best of intentions, do they? It's a nice weeding-out process."

RIGHT: The eagerly
awaited second album,
entitled *Fearless*.

OPPOSITE: Taylor with her
award for Favorite Country
Female Artist at the American
Music Awards in 2008.

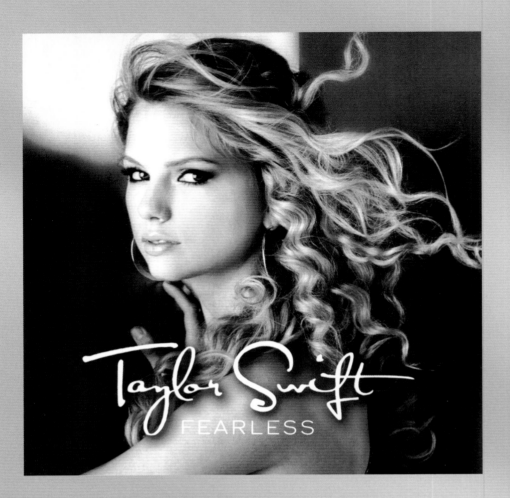

SHE WHO DARES

Follow-up albums are usually tough for artists. The debut release is crammed with years of material, while the sophomore effort has to be produced during a period of intense activity—touring, promotions, video production, media training—all the things new artists go through on their way to the top. But Swift's knack for writing songs of the moment meant she always had new material. Her "normal" life at high school and subsequent experiences in showbiz gave her great inspiration. Her songs struck the right chords not just with fans her own age, but with critics in the usually cynical music press. And if she was now mixing with celebrities, then that new world would also be reported back on in Swift's songs. Her honesty about her life wasn't limited to Pennsylvania, Hendersonville, or high school.

It was clear that Taylor Swift's *Fearless* was going to be a step up even from her multiplatinum debut album. Just after Big Machine Records released the first single from the second record, "Love Story," another Swift love song from *Fearless*, "White Horse," was played on the season premiere of top TV medical drama show *Grey's Anatomy* on September 25, 2008. "The song 'White Horse' is written about that moment where you realize that the guy that you thought was your Prince Charming really isn't," she told www.countryhound.com.

On November 11, 2008, *Fearless* hit the streets. The reaction from fans and music buyers was phenomenal. The album immediately took the top spot on the *Billboard* Hot 200 chart, selling an incredible 592,000 copies in its first week, according to Nielsen SoundScan. And just to prove that Nashville really did have a new star to match Shania Twain, Garth Brooks, and the Dixie Chicks, the record was the highest placed debut of any country album that year.

It was a major step forward from *Taylor Swift*. The singer-songwriter was more hands-on in the control room during the making of *Fearless*, earning a producer credit. The songs, while still rooted in teenage high school soap opera, were more

"I still like to live in a **whimsical world** that seems more romantic and fantasy-related because real life seems *so hard*"

PREVIOUS PAGES: A live
performance during the
American Music Awards
in Los Angeles, 2008.

RIGHT: Taylor at the 51st
Annual Grammy Awards
MusicCares Signings
Day 3 in 2009.

OPPOSITE: Swift performing
at the Sound Relief concert
in Sydney in 2009, in
aid of the victims of the
bushfire in Victoria and
the floods in Queensland.

sophisticated and better crafted but still immediate. All the tracks were culled from her diary of real life events and from the heart, her stock in trade.

The overall sound on *Fearless* is top-quality country pop with producer Chapman again showcasing his ability to make country music palatable to the Disney generation, while retaining enough tradition in the arrangements to woo older country fans, thus making no apology for Taylor's natural county twang. Lyrically the new release was a cut above songs by many more seasoned country songwriters. While her songs deal with puppy love and first heartbreaks, they do so with pithy simplicity and with words and music somehow always in sync emotionally and musically. If that isn't the sign of an instinctive songsmith, then what is?

ALL ALONE

The first single, "Love Story," showed that Swift's songwriting talents on the debut album were no fluke. Here was a genuine Nashville songwriter with pop rock crossover potential whose writing was even more accomplished and mature thanks to a year or so of maturity and development. Of the thirteen songs on *Fearless*, Swift co-wrote or wrote all of them; seven of them were Swift solo efforts. Swift

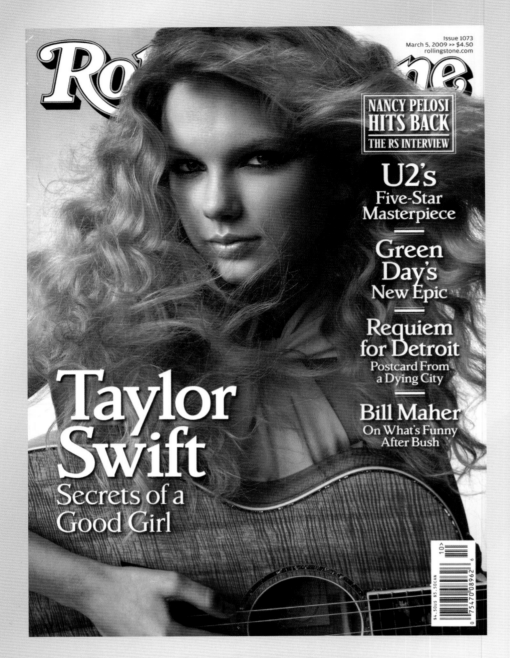

said, ". . . for *Fearless*, I was on the road, that was my job—on the road nonstop—and so when I would get a great idea for a song, I didn't have anybody around to write it with; I just wrote it myself."

Swift was taking country music to a new level. While established superstars talked about country music being based on honesty and integrity, there was still an accepted privacy line that artists and writers did not cross. For the young Swift, however, still innocent enough to think nothing of letting the world hear her teenage diary entries in her songs, that line seemed to have been erased. Music fans have always enjoyed analyzing the lyrics by their favorite songwriter, drawing conclusions on how much of the song relates precisely to the star's personal life. Never before had a country singer been so transparent.

This was Taylor's world. The MySpace, Facebook, Twitter world of immediacy, interaction, and sharing was perfectly encapsulated in her burgeoning music career. She posted songs online, and she blogged about events in her life, some serious, some trivial. And her songs were musical extensions of those online posts. "When you buy my album you are going to find out what I've gone through in the past two years. And you'll probably be able to figure out how many breakups I've gone through, how many people I've fallen for—it's very autobiographical."

THE FAN CLUB GROWS

She won the prestigious NSAI Songwriter/Artist of the Year Award in 2009, the same award she tied Alan Jackson for in 2007, which offered proof that Nashville's writing community understood and recognized that Swift was a rare talent, one to be appreciated and respected. Multiple NSAI award winner Jeffrey Steele, one of the most prolific and admired songwriters in Music City, called her "one of the most promising songwriters to pop up in Nashville in a long, long time." Sure, there were some music business balloon poppers casting doubt on Swift's talent, putting her success down to social media marketing, much as they had with Garth and Shania in the past. But those in the know were lining up behind Swift. Noted songwriter Dolly Parton told TV's Larry King that Taylor had a "good head on her shoulders. She's surrounded with wonderful people. Her songs are great. She keeps herself anchored. She knows who she is, and she's living and standing by that."

John Rich, co-writer of "The Way I Love You," possibly the strongest song on *Fearless*, and half of the genre-stretching country duo Big and Rich enjoys a reputation as one of the most commercial hit writers and producers in Nashville (Gretchen Wilson, Keith Anderson, and Jason Aldean are among his satisfied clients). Rich called her "one of those incredible natural talents that comes down the pike once in a while." Tanya Tucker, who topped the country charts when she was just thirteen years old with the song "Delta Dawn" back in the 1970s, recognized genuine talent in Swift immediately. "She has that quality that the superstars have. She's driven, personable, approachable, and a fine songwriter. She's gonna be around a long, long time."

LEFT: The platinum edition of Taylor's second hit album, *Fearless*.

DOLLY PARTON

WHEN a journalist compared Taylor Swift to Dolly Parton, Taylor was genuinely flattered. "That's a really awesome compliment because Dolly has a catalog of over eight hundred songs that she's written and she's really witty, she's got a quick wit."

Swift then told the journalist: "I heard a story about her once, there's always that moment in your concerts when you're playing an acoustic song or something and it's a really quiet moment and some guy in the back is like, 'I love you Dolly!'

"She just looked up from her song and said, 'I thought I told you to stay in the truck'—just really quick. I have just loved her ever since I first heard her."

An astute observer of country music's ups and downs since she first took the Opry stage in the 1960s, Dolly Parton is a Taylor Swift fan too, it seems. The country music legend had plenty of positives to say when asked about the teen sensation on CNN's *Larry King Live* show in November 2010. "She's got the qualities that could last a long time. I'm hoping that she's just having a really, really hot streak. I hope her fifteen minutes of fame lasts for forty years, and it very well might."

Those were sincere words from a veteran artist who has never been one to hitch herself to Nashville's latest and greatest unless genuinely impressed by them. Dolly Parton, still probably the best-known country music singer in the world, has one of the most impressive résumés in pop music history. One of the first country stars to cross over into pop music and then the mainstream entertainment world, she's also a successful businesswoman with her own theme park, a restaurant franchise owner, a longtime TV star, a multi-award-winning recording artist, and, arguably most significantly, a naturally gifted hit songwriter.

Dolly is the most honored female country performer of all time (although Taylor's catching up fast). She has had twenty–five songs go to number one on the *Billboard* country charts, scored more than forty career top ten country albums, and charted more than one hundred singles. As far as honors go, she's won a modest seven Grammy awards, ten Country Music Association awards, five Academy of Country Music awards, and three American Music Awards, and she is one of only seven female artists to win the Country Music Association's Entertainer of the Year Award (the others being Loretta Lynn, Shania Twain, Reba McEntire, the Dixie Chicks, Barbara Mandrell, and, of course, Taylor Swift).

Raised dirt poor in a log cabin in the eastern Tennessee mountains at Locust Ridge, near Sevierville, Parton turned to music as a young girl for entertainment. She somehow acquired a guitar at eight years old and by eleven was singing around town and appearing on a local Knoxville radio station. As soon as she was old enough she graduated high school and headed to Nashville. In just two years she had a record deal and in 1967 a promising single on country radio, the prophetic and heavily ironic "Dumb Blonde."

When country star Porter Wagoner needed a female singer for his syndicated television show, Dolly got the gig and became a household name in no time at all. Larger than life from the outset and always willing to play up the dumb blonde image—"it takes a lot of money to look this cheap" is a favorite Dolly line—her songwriting established her as a bona fide talent. And with songs like "Jolene" and "Coat of Many Colors" outshining Wagoner, she had no real option but to go solo, which she did in 1974. She wrote a song about their split, "I Will Always Love You," that would make her a small fortune over the next thirty years, especially when Whitney Houston got her hands on it.

In 1977 Dolly completely crossed over into the mainstream world with the smash hit "Here You Come Again." "I'm not leaving country," she said at the time. "I'm just taking it with me." She went Hollywood with the 1980 hit comedy movie *9 to 5*, earning rave reviews for her performance and an Oscar nomination for writing the title song.

Dolly has also devoted time to giving back. The Dolly Parton Imagination Library was set up to give every preschool child a book every month until they reach kindergarten. With the help of local sponsors, this program has expanded to more than eight hundred communities in forty-one states in the United States and is giving away more than 5 million books a year. Dolly said, "My dad was prouder of me for this program than for my music career. He thought it was grand that all the kids called me the Book Lady."

OPPOSITE: Dolly Parton performing in Chicago in 1977.

WHAT DID THEY SAY?

Reviews for *Fearless* were mostly favorable. *All Music Guide* was clearly impressed, saying: "Despite the success of her self-titled 2006 debut, there's nothing at all diva-like about Swift on 2008's *Fearless*: she's soft-spoken and considerate, a big sister instead of a big star. Nowhere is this truer than on 'Fifteen,' a kind warning for a teen to watch her heart, sung from the perspective of a woman who's perhaps twice that age—a sly trick for the eighteen-year-old."

The American Music Channel called it "the best example of contemporary, hip country since Shania teamed up with Mutt Lange."

Trade magazine *Billboard* talked about the "genius and accessibility" of *Fearless*, while rock'n'roll bible *Rolling Stone* described it as "so rigorously crafted it sounds like it has been scientifically engineered in a hit factory—with confessions that are squirmingly intimate and true." "Love Story," the first single from the album, gave Swift her first top five on the pop charts and her third country number one. The song would also go Top Ten in the United Kingdom, the first time a country artist had managed that since Shania five years earlier. The song also went to number one in Australia and number three in New Zealand. It was a sign not only that Taylor had the potential to find stardom in America, but that the world really was her oyster. Global success would follow, and very quickly.

ABOVE: An assured Taylor Swift giving another great performance at the CMA Music Festival in 2008.

In America, *Fearless* sat at the top of the *Billboard* 200 for ten straight weeks, eventually topping the chart for thirty–five weeks (although not consecutively).

Hot on the heels of the album's launch and Taylor's whirlwind of TV, print, and radio interviews to promote it were the 2008 CMA Awards. The honors wouldn't be Taylor's this year, but she would get to perform and present, and, more than that, she would meet her idol Shania Twain. For all the massive record sales, glowing reviews, celebrity parties, Hollywood friendships, romances, and industry awards, Taylor Swift was still a teenage girl, just like the millions who came to her Web sites. And when it came to the star-studded CMAs, she was still a fan herself.

Taylor headlined her post-CMA blog post on November 14 "I Met Shania Twain and it was AWESOME." Below the underlined title, she gushed that she couldn't believe it when Shania Twain actually came up to introduce herself and told her she was doing a great job. She told her fans that Shania really was as beautiful as they might imagine and that she was completely starstruck. She also admitted that she was left in tears when Shania walked away and how great she felt about being a country music fan and proud to be a country music artist.

And if she lost to Carrie Underwood for the Best Country Female award at the CMAs, the American Music Awards the same month corrected that omission by naming Taylor their best country female. Quite rightly, Taylor thanked her fans on her MySpace page, something she was becoming quite practiced at.

FEARLESSLY GOING . . .

The year 2009 was building beautifully for Taylor Swift. She was doing as well as any new country music artist could, and far better than most in Nashville during a time of record sale recession. According to the Nielsen SoundScan report, country music album sales dropped 24 percent in 2008 from the previous year's numbers and in 2009 dropped even more. Nashville sales were propped up by Taylor Swift's multiplatinum albums.

Most of the year would be spent touring. In January 2009, Swift announced her North American Fearless Tour, planned for fifty–two cities in thirty–eight states and provinces in the United States and Canada over the span of six months. But there was also time for some prestigious one-off events, some alone, some with her music friends.

In January 2009 Swift became the youngest country music artist to make a musical guest appearance on the legendary comedy show *Saturday Night Live*. On February 8, 2009, Swift performed her song "Fifteen" with Miley Cyrus at the fifty-first Grammy Awards.

The Academy of Country Music, typically slightly more progressive than the more conservative CMAs, gave Taylor an award for Album of the Year. She was the youngest artist in history to receive the honor. Visibly emotional, she said: "If you've ever talked to me for more than five minutes, then I'm going to write a song about you. I'd like to thank all of the characters in my songs, Abigail, Tim McGraw, and Romeo!" She was singlehandedly taking country music into a new, uncharted (for Nashville) youth market. The same month as she won the AMC best album award it was reported that Taylor Swift had sold more than 14 million downloads. Having crossed over from country to pop—with deceptive ease, it might be added—Taylor was now breathing the same rarified pop air as her musical heroes Garth Brooks and Shania Twain. The signs were good that she could also match them for global success, with the decent chart placing of "Love Story" around the world.

The fifty–two-city Fearless tour kicked off in spring of 2009 with opening acts Kellie Pickler and Gloriana. The rush for tickets was insane, with Staples Center tickets selling out in just two minutes. Aware that America loved Taylor, Big Machine and Team Taylor decided to check out the international picture.

There would be some UK dates built into the initial part of the tour, dates set up to test the international waters and see what a British audience, who Big Machine knew had loved Shania, would make of their artist. They needn't have worried as Swift was quickly embraced by international fans and critics. The *Guardian* newspaper was cautious but positive, commenting that though "her regulation blond bounciness and bubbly ditties about high-school Romeos make her deceptively similar to the likes of Miley Cyrus—there is also the matter of her gushing about our 'adorable accents'—it seems Swift really cares about what she's doing."

Esteemed BBC Radio presenter and veteran music critic Bob Harris told the same newspaper that she had what it took to last: "Nashville has a way of producing artists whose career lasts a long time. There's an expectation that those artists will deliver top ten albums over a ten- or fifteen-year period." After the initial May reconnaissance trip to England, Swift returned in late summer to play a couple of sets at the rock-oriented V Festival. In the past when Nashville acts tiptoed into British waters they had been barraged with redneck, hillbilly, and cowboy hat jokes. Not so Taylor, who, on a bill with the Script, Lily Allen, and Pixie Lott had the Brits singing along and embracing the integrity and pure pop approach of her music.

The year 2009 was looking even better than the phenomenal breakthrough year of 2008. Critics were mostly won over, the media loved her, and the fans were not just buying albums and downloads by the million but actively joining the Taylor community. Everything Taylor touched seemed to turn to gold, or in the case of her record sales, platinum. What could possibly go wrong?

SHANIA TWAIN

O F all the artists who have influenced Taylor Swift, both as a young kid learning about country and as an adult star figuring out the music business, Shania Twain has arguably had the greatest impact. Taylor called the Canadian superstar "the most impressive and independent and confident and successful female artist to ever hit country music" and blogged that she was "the reason I wanted to do this in the first place."

She told *Time* magazine, "She [Shania] was just so strong and so independent and wrote all her own songs. That meant so much to me, even as a ten-year-old. Just knowing that the stories she was telling in those songs—those were her stories."

If you're going to learn from anyone, it may as well be the best. For sheer impact and commercial success very few artists in the history of music, let alone country music, come close to Shania's monumental achievements. Her *Come on Over* album is the best-selling album by a female artist ever, at around 39 million copies—and counting—sold around the world.

Shania, whose real name was Eilleen, was born in 1965 and started singing when she was a young girl. Unlike Taylor, the young Shania performed as a way of making a few extra dollars for her family. She grew up poor in Timmins, Ontario, Canada and sang for most of her formative years, eventually fronting a pretty good local cover band, and getting noticed by people who could help her career in music. She made some demos and trips to Nashville, and things were looking more than promising when tragedy interrupted her plans for a future as a recording artist.

On November 1, 1987, Twain's mother and adoptive father were killed in a car crash. Shania became the head of the family and devoted her time to them, singing in a local resort to keep food on the table. These traumatic events may have delayed Shania's rise to the top, but she learned important values, such as emotional strength and fortitude, that have helped in her later career.

In the early 1990s she signed with Mercury Records in Nashville and changed her name to Shania (it means "I'm on my way" in Ojibwa Indian). Her self-titled debut album came out in 1993 with little fanfare, but it contained a couple of minor hits.

That summer something happened that vaulted Shania from being just one of many promising acts in Nashville to a superstar in waiting. While working in the studio in London, record producer Mutt Lange saw Shania's first video on CMT Europe. Although Lange was best known for his intrinsically commercial stadium rock production work with bands like AC/DC and—another Taylor top pick—Def Leppard, he was a country music fan. He was drawn to Shania's voice and style. Lange tracked her down and they married later that year. Shania really was on her way.

Mutt produced and co-wrote songs with Shania for her follow-up album, *The Woman in Me*. The record was an immediate success and gave Shania her first number 1 single, "Any Man of Mine." *Come on Over*, the album that followed, launched Shania as a world star. It was crammed with hits like "You're Still the One," "Don't Be Stupid," "You've Got a Way," "Man! I Feel Like a Woman!" "That Don't Impress Me Much," and "From This Moment On."

The album broke Shania internationally and went to number one on the UK album charts—and stayed there for an incredible eleven weeks, selling more than four million copies. It was a similar story in other countries. Shania gracefully became a pop star while never rejecting her country roots. Like Taylor Swift fifteen years later, she was seen as a music star, not a country music star, and for the next ten years was one of the biggest acts in the world. Her last studio album *Up* was released in 2002, but she remains one of the biggest names in music, something Taylor Swift remarked on in 2009 when discussing Shania at a Canadian press conference. "Every single award show it was, 'Where's Shania? When's she gonna come back? When's she gonna put out something new?' The fact that she's so memorable means she's done such an incredible job at really implementing herself in country music to where she's never, ever gonna be gone. And I love that.

"Shania's absolutely my favorite because she's so memorable. I'm always just gonna be so, so in love with what she's done for country music. You know, as far as any other artist, when you leave a genre and leave the music industry for that long, people would forget you—but not Shania. No one ever forgot her."

OPPOSITE: The hugely successful Shania Twain has been one of Taylor's most important influences.

6

Meet Kanye West

DUBBED the "Oscars for Youth," MTV's Video Music Awards (VMAs) have become the most influential awards and TV event on the pop calendar since the mid-1980s. More hip than the Grammys or AMAs and certainly more influential than the CMAs or ACMs in breaking a new country artist worldwide, 2009's VMAs were especially significant to Big Machine and Taylor Swift, who was nominated for the Best Female Video award for her song "You Belong with Me." It was a momentous achievement and a possible turning point in a new artist's career. No TV show enjoyed as much intense media focus or had as much potential for significant cultural impact as the VMAs.

Ever since Madonna grabbed the headlines at the very first VMAs in 1984, popping out of a wedding cake in a revealing white lace bustier with stockings for a provocative version of "Like a Virgin," the VMAs had witnessed a series of controversial, outrageous, musically significant, and always headline-grabbing incidents. This one was to be no different, if more regrettable.

The 2009 VMAs were held at the historic Radio City Music Hall in New York and hosted once more by controversial British comedian Russell Brand, who had grabbed a few headlines himself the previous year for some quips about the Jonas Brothers. After a snappy rendition of "You Belong with Me," Taylor was presented with the Best Female Video Award by Shakira and Taylor Lautner. It was a perfect moment. Swift had performed at the top of her game, and now she had the chance to show the watching world the fizzy likability and down-home charm that had won her an army of devoted fans. Well practiced at acceptance speeches, especially for one so young and new to the business, this was her chance to speak to the whole world.

As she was about to do that exactly that, something happened that, in the moment, was shocking and difficult, although ultimately it would see Taylor reach the world's press with global headlines that could never be matched by even the most audacious publicity stunt. And best of all, Taylor would earn sympathy and admiration for her part in it. She was absolutely the innocent party as the larger-than-life Kanye West bizarrely jumped up on stage and interrupted the slightly nervous Taylor, who had just cleared her throat and said, "I sing country music, so thank you so much for giving me a chance to win a VMA."

Kanye West then grabbed her microphone and said to a stunned live and TV audience: "Yo, Tay [sic], I'm really happy for you and I'mma let you finish, but Beyoncé had one of the best videos of all time. One of the best videos of all time!" Cameras cut to a shocked and embarrassed Beyoncé. Swift, clearly shocked, looked down at the floor and began to walk away. The audience then booed Kanye after he ended his rant, flipped off the room, and stormed off backstage.

Elliott Wilson, founder and chief executive officer of Rap Radar, was sitting close to the Kanye West entourage during the ceremony and spoke to CNN.com about the incident: "At first, people weren't sure if it was kind of like a gag," he said. "You could feel everybody being nervous and not knowing if it was a prank or something. Then people started booing him really loud. The reaction to his tantrum was so strong . . . and what happened was, he gave everybody the finger."

Rebellious singer Pink was none too pleased, and according to MTV shook her head in disapproval at Kanye before he was ushered away by security. Her reaction was indicative of the music and celebrity community. Showing class and wisdom, Beyoncé, when she later won Video of the Year, had Taylor come up onstage to finally say her few words of acceptance for her award. Swift walked onstage and said, "Maybe we could try this again," to a huge ovation.

THE PEOPLE VOTED!

Subsequently, West would be pilloried for days, even weeks, to come, but Taylor would be acclaimed as the innocent victim in a scandal that would reach as far as the White House. This being the age of instant comment, celebrities started making their feelings known. Pink tweeted, "Kanye West is the biggest piece of [expletive] on earth. Quote me." Joel Madden of the rock band Good Charlotte tweeted, "WOW, Taylor Swift's first VMA and she didn't even get to ENJOY it! Kanye, you were a bully on that one man."

Celebrity blogger Perez Hilton tweeted, "Taylor Swift deserved that award, damnit. It is what THE PEOPLE voted! My heart broke for her, she looked so sad at the end of that moment."

Singer Katy Perry weighed in with "F--- u Kanye. It's like you stepped on a kitten."

VMA nominee Kelly Clarkson wrote a letter to Kanye on her blog, saying: "What happened to you as a child?? Did you not get hugged enough?"

But that was just the beginning of the affair. The following day, a CNBC reporter about to interview President Barack Obama asked if the president's daughters had been upset by Kanye West interrupting Taylor Swift at the VMAs. When audio of the president's off-the-record answer hit the Internet, media frenzy barely described the furor. Obama said: "I thought that was really inappropriate. You know, it was like, she's getting an award and what are you butting in? . . . The young lady seems like a perfectly nice person, she's getting her award and what's he doing up there? He's a jackass."

And if that wasn't enough, Kanye was next criticized by another president of the United States, Jimmy Carter, who said Kanye's actions were "completely uncalled for."

Kanye attempted to make amends with an apology on his blog, writing: "I feel like Ben Stiller in *Meet the Parents* when he messed up everything and Robert De Niro asked him to leave . . . That was Taylor's moment and I had no right in any way to take it from her. I am truly sorry." West then went on the *Jay Leno Show* that night to attempt some damage control.

RIGHT: As the controversy over Kanye West's comments grew, it became a national talking point. Here, Kanye and Taylor's faces have been carved into a pumpkin.

JAY LENO: Have a seat, my friend. First of all, let me say thank you for honoring this commitment. A lot of times, people—things happen. They kind of back out at the last minute, or they have a publicist or someone call and say, "Oh, I'm sorry, my client's not available." So thank you for coming and doing this, in light of all the things that have been going on. Tell me about your day. Have you had a tough day today? (*Laughter.*)

KANYE WEST: Yeah, it's been extremely difficult. I just—just dealing with the fact that I hurt someone or took anything away, you know, from a talented artist or from anyone, because I only wanted to help people. My entire life, I've only wanted to give and do something that I felt was right. And I immediately knew in the situation that it was wrong, and it wasn't a spectacle or just—you know, it's actually someone's emotions, you know, that I stepped on. And it was very—it was just—it was rude, period. And, you know, I'd like to be able to apologize to her in person. And I wanted to—

JAY LENO: So when did you know you were wrong? Was it afterwards? As you were doing it? When did it strike you, "Uh-oh"?

KANYE WEST: As soon as I gave the mike back to her and she didn't keep going. (*Laughter.*)

JAY LENO: Let me ask you something. I was fortunate enough to meet your mom and talk with your mom a number of years ago. What do you think she would have said about this? Would she be disappointed in this? Would she give you a lecture?

KANYE WEST: Yeah. You know, obviously, you know, I deal with hurt. And, you know, so many celebrities, they never take the time off. I've never taken the time off to really—you know, just music after music and tour after tour. I'm just ashamed that my hurt caused someone else's hurt. My dream of what awards shows are supposed to be, 'cause—and I don't try to justify it because I was just in the wrong. That's period. But I need to, after this, take some time off and just analyze how I'm going to make it through the rest of this life, how I'm going to improve. Because I am a celebrity, and that's something I have to deal with. And if there's anything I could do to help Taylor in the future or help anyone, I'd like—you know, I want to live this thing. It's hard sometimes, so—

JAY LENO: Thanks for coming here, and thanks for doing that.

RIGHT: The star styled an American idol on the cover of the *New York Times Style* magazine in 2009.

PREVIOUS PAGES: Taylor performing onstage at a sold-out Madison Square Gardens show, New York, 2009.

american idols
HOLIDAY 2009
The singer Taylor Swift

KANYEGATE AND *SNL*

On September 15, 2009, just two days after the outburst, Taylor Swift appeared on the popular morning TV show *The View*. Naturally she was asked about Kanye West's actions. "Well, I think my overall thought process was something like, 'Wow, I can't believe I won, this is awesome, don't trip and fall, I'm going to get to thank the fans, this is so cool. Oh, Kanye West is here. Cool haircut. What are you doing there?' And then, 'Ouch.' And then, 'I guess I'm not gonna get to thank the fans.'"

Taylor also admitted that she was physically and emotionally shaken by the events: "You know, I'm not gonna say that I wasn't rattled by it, but I had to perform live five minutes later, so I had to get myself back to the place where I could perform."

After Taylor spoke to America on *The View*, Kanye West contacted her to apologize personally. His spokesperson stated: "After the show he spoke personally to the country music superstar via telephone and has apologized to the nineteen-year-old singer. She has accepted Mr. West's apology. The contents of the phone call are to remain private." Later Swift told ABC News Radio: "He was very sincere in his apology and I accepted that apology."

Once the incident died down a little Taylor was able to feel and acknowledge the acceptance and respect she had found in the music and entertainment community. "There were a lot of people around me backstage that were saying wonderful, incredible things and just having my back," she said. "I just never imagined that there were that many people looking out for me."

The cultural impact of what came to be called "KanyeGate" was massive. Taylor Swift, a promising young country singer and songwriter, overnight became a

BELOW: Taylor's poise and grace was praised following the Kanye incident.

LITTLE MISS *Sunshine*

TAYLOR SWIFT, COUNTRY MUSIC DARLIN', WINS THE PRIZE FOR GRACE UNDER PRESSURE.

Interview by LYNN HIRSCHBERG *Photographs by* RAYMOND MEIER

... grew up in Pennsylvania, and yet you fell in love with country music at a young age. What did you hear that attracted you to country?

LeAnn Rimes. I heard "Blue" by LeAnn Rimes, and that song resonated with me. It was nine years ago. She was young — around 14 — and I was about 10 when I heard it and she was doing these things that I could only dream about doing. There was something just so motivating about that.

Did you know what, or where, Nashville was?

I was watching a special on TV about the singer Faith Hill, and she talked about how she went to Nashville. That's the moment that I realized that Nashville is where you need to be if you want to sing country music. And so every day I would beg my parents nonstop: "We need to go to Nashville. Can we please go to Nashville?" When I was 11, we went during spring break. I had been singing karaoke and I competed in karaoke competitions. So, I had this little demo CD of me singing karaoke music, and my mom would pull up outside one of the record labels on Music Row in Nashville and I would run in and say to the receptionist, "Hi, I'm Taylor. I'm 11. I want a record deal. Call me."

Did you wear a cowboy hat?

No. My hair was always too big for that. I wore jeans and probably some sort of sparkly shirt.

How did your classmates regard your music?

I didn't really have that many friends at school. Kids would just heckle me: "Oh, go sing that country *beep*." It just dawned on me that I had to love being different or else I was going to end up being dark and angry and frustrated by school. Sometimes I felt like I was some sort of spy because I would go to school during the day, and then, after school, I had this life that was completely different. I definitely was

more nervous walking into my first day of freshman year in high school than I was walking up to record labels and handing them my CD. In school, I learned to stop talking about music because they didn't like it when I did. I led a double life. I kind of started to live in fear when I would sing the national anthem at the 76ers game. If there was a write-up about it the next day in our local paper, I knew it was gonna be a bad day at school for me.

Your mother loved Def Leppard. She played that nonstop when she was pregnant with you.

I love Def Leppard! It's comforting for me to listen to them. I love a great song. If that great song is by 50 Cent, I'll listen to it.

You started writing songs when you were 12, and nearly all your songs are autobiographical. Was that a way of coping with being an outsider at school?

Absolutely. I would sit on the edge of class and watch people interact with each other. I'd watch guys flirt with cool girls and I would watch best friends talk, and I would go home and write about it. If you listen to my albums, it's like reading my diary.

And you always use real names in your songs.

I don't hesitate — people who have no idea that I have a crush on them won't find out through me telling them, but they will find out when they hear their name in a song. There was this guy who opened a couple of shows for me on tour and I talked to him a couple of times, but he never knew that I liked him. So I wrote this song called "Hey Stephen," and when my album came out, I sent him a text message: "Hey, Track 5." It was so funny. He sent me back a long e-mail saying, "Oh, my God!"

You recently finished filming a movie called "Valentine's Day." Did you like acting?

Yes, but it's a small part. I play the kind of girl I didn't like in high school. She's forced to go to gym class and doesn't want to be there. The director, Garry Marshall, was wonderful — and both of our lucky numbers are 13, so we talked about that most of the time.

Do you still sing karaoke?

No. But if I were to do karaoke, it would probably be something from "Grease." I'd sing "You're the One That I Want" — or Def Leppard. Whenever I hear Def Leppard, I just freak out. ∎

TAYLOR SWIFT CHATS WITH T'S EDITOR AT LARGE, LYNN HIRSCHBERG, IN AN EXCLUSIVE SCREEN TEST. GO TO NYTIMES.COM/TMAGAZINE.

household name. For those new to Taylor who watched the proceedings on TV, she became a figure of interest and much sympathy. Anyone who missed the broadcast could not avoid the subsequent media saturation, especially once the president of the United States became inadvertently involved.

It didn't harm record sales either, with Big Machine head honcho Scott Borchetta later admitting to National Public Radio that the incident "did end up being a positive in her career in terms of name recognition." Anyone who knew Taylor or had just seen through her songs how she rarely allowed anyone to hurt her without comment knew that the singer would have her say, once she'd had time to reflect and consider.

That opportunity came quickly when she guest–hosted *Saturday Night Live* and wrote her opening monologue.

"Oh! Thank you! Oh, thank you so much! It's great to be here hosting Saturday Night Live! I have wanted to host this show . . . ever since I was a little kid, staying up past my bedtime to watch Bill Hader and Andy Samberg.

"Being here is incredible. I'm excited, and I'm nervous, and, you know, whenever I'm feeling strong emotions about something like this . . . I usually write a song about it. So this is what I came up with. It's called 'Monologue Song.'

> "I like glitter and sparkly dresses
> but I'm not going to talk about that . . . in my monologue.
> I like baking and things that smell like winter
> but I'm not going to talk about that . . . in my monologue.
>
> "I like writing songs about douchebags who cheat on me
> but I'm not gonna say that . . . in my monologue.
> I like writing their names into songs so they are ashamed to go in public
> but I'm not gonna say that . . . in my monologue.
> This is . . . my musical monologue.
>
> "You might think I'd bring up Joe, that guy who
>   broke up with me on the phone
> but I'm not going to mention him . . . in my monologue.
> 'Hey, Joe! I'm doing really well! I'm hosting *SNL*!'
> But I'm not gonna talk about that . . . in my monologue.

RIGHT: A baby elephant signed by Taylor for an AIDS charity helping orphans in Africa.

ABOVE: Taylor showing her sense of humor, appearing on *Saturday Night Live*.

"And if you're wondering if I might be dating the werewolf from Twilight
[*mouths 'Hey, Taylor'; blows kiss; winks*]
I'm not gonna comment on that . . . in my monologue.
This is . . . my musical monologue.

"You might be expecting me to say something bad about Kanye,
and how he ran up on the stage and ruined my VMA monologue.
But there's nothing more to say, 'cause everything is okay
I've got security lining the stage in my *SNL* monologue!"

By the fall of 2009, Taylor Swift had seen the good, the bad, and the ugly of the entertainment business, and dealt admirably with the kind of intense media attention usually reserved for the most major of celebrities. If she was feeling even a little disenchanted with life at the top, something more music related and quite phenomenal was just around the corner to cheer her up. Taylor Swift was about to make history again.

GREASE

WHEN Taylor Swift caught the acting bug and joined a children's theater group in Pennsylvania, she was discovering her acting and performing skills as well as defining the kind of music she'd devote her energy and career to. She told GAC TV: "I was playing the role of Sandy in *Grease* and it just came out sounding country. It was all I had listened to, so I guess it was just kind of natural. I decided country music was what I needed to be doing."

The universally popular *Grease*, which most people know from the smash John Travolta and Olivia Newton-John movie of 1978, started out as a stage musical written by Jim Jacobs (a 1950s greaser) and Warren Casey (a former high school teacher in the 1950s). The story focuses on Sandy, the goody-two-shoes nice girl, and her summer romance with wild boy greaser (hence the name of the show) Danny. It was going to recapture teen life in the pre-Vietnam, more innocent and fun-loving 1950s, as Jim Jacobs explained: "Harking back to a lifestyle that seemed centered on hairstyles (oily, gooey, coiffs), the food (cheap, fatty, hamburgers and soggy fries) and cool custom cars (more gunk and sludge) or any and all things 'greasy.' I suggested we call it *Grease*."

The authors initially created a work that reveled in real 1950s youth culture and was pretty hard hitting, as it focused on tough issues like teen pregnancy and gang warfare. Set in a fictional high school, the musical features a group of typical teens working out their romances, fights, hopes, dreams, and growing pains to a rock'n'roll soundtrack. Over the years the show has mellowed and become a more family-oriented musical while retaining the romance and great songs of the original.

The show opened on February 14, 1972, in New York. Within six months a national tour crossed the United States and Canada with a young John Travolta (Danny Zuko in the movie) as Doody, a nerdy kid who idolizes tough guy Danny. It opened in Australia and England (with a very young Richard Gere as Danny) before becoming a worldwide smash. By the time the movie came around in 1978, John Travolta had graduated to become leading man opposite squeaky-clean Australian pop star Olivia Newton-John. Olivia Newton-John was just starting out in showbiz and was pretty much untried as an actor. She had been in the surreal sci-fi movie *Toomorrow*, a project from Don Kirshner, the man behind the music '60s pop superstars The Monkees. But the film was a miss at the box office and Newton John was determined to get herself into *Grease*, screen testing successfully and winning the part of a lifetime. A role, incidentally, that Marie Osmond allegedly turned down because she opposed the part where Sandy turned "bad girl."

The movie takes advantage of some genuine onscreen chemistry between Travolta and Newton-John as they tell the story of how Danny and Sandy first met one summer on the beach and on return to school discover they are from very different worlds. Danny is the leader of the T-Birds, a greaser biker gang, while Sandy is part of the ultra straight and girly Pink Ladies group. Sandy doesn't know want to make of the tough guy Danny, who'd seemed so sweet during their summer fling. Danny in turn struggles to show his tender side in front of his macho gang pals.

The movie was the highest grossing film of 1978 in America and the soundtrack album, filled with 1950s-style songs, was the second biggest-selling album in the U.S. It was only beaten by the soundtrack album from another musical classic, *Staying Alive*, featuring the music of the Bee Gees and starring a certain John Travolta in the lead role!

Revived in New York in 2007, *Grease* is now the thirteenth longest-running show in Broadway history. There are times when Taylor looks (and sounds) for all the world as if she's still playing Sandy, the good girl with a romantic heart and an eye for a bad boy gone straight. The ever modest and humble Taylor says she only got the lead roles in shows like *Grease* as a kid because she was tallest of her group. Anyone who has seen her videos, live shows, movies, and TV appearances might beg to differ, though, and acknowledge that Taylor's acting teachers knew more than she realized!

OPPOSITE: The stars of *Grease*, Olivia Newton-John and John Travolta, in an iconic scene from the film.

7

Today was a

Fairytale

DOWNTOWN'S Lower Broadway is Nashville's most historic and vibrant street. Fifth Avenue crosses Broadway, and about a hundred yards up the hill sits the grand and dignified Ryman Auditorium, once the regular venue of the legendary Grand Ole Opry radio show and still the spiritual home of country music. Across from the Ryman's side parking lot, where trucks park to load in equipment and artists gather for a smoke before a concert, is a nondescript, unmarked back door into one of the most colorful and significant honky-tonks in Nashville.

Those who know the way in through the door find themselves in the upstairs back bar of the Tootsie Orchid Lounge, the most revered bar in country music. It's a wild and crazy place; open day and night from Sunday to Sunday, in the past it has given refreshment, respite, and inspiration to country superstars like Willie Nelson, Kris Kristofferson, and Taylor's heroine, 1950s great Patsy Cline.

Country superstars in the good old days loved the bar's proximity to the Ryman (which was dry and served no alcohol), and Tootsie's became the watering hole for generations of country legends. Walk through the back bar to the tiny wooden-floored front area and you'll invariably find a heaving crowd, bopping to whichever Haggard or Jones tune the band (who'll be playing in the tiny front window space by the front door) has just launched into. Go out the door and you're on Broadway, staring at the new face of country music, the purpose-built downtown music venue, the Bridgestone Arena.

PREVIOUS PAGE: The young star onstage at the CMA Music Festival, Nashville, 2009.

OPPOSITE: Taylor surrounded by adoring fans onstage during the Country Music Awards in Nashville, 2009.

BELOW: Downtown Nashville where visitors can find the honky-tonks and world famous Tootsie's Orchid Lounge.

BELOW RIGHT: The modern Bridgestone Arena in Nashville.

Back in 2009, the Bridgestone was called the Sommet Center, which had been home of country music's biggest night, the CMA Awards, since the show outgrew the Opry House, where it had been based since the ceremonies began in 1967. Downtown Nashville comes to a stop for CMA Awards night. Roads are closed and barricades are set up by police to maintain security and keep fans away from the arriving celebrities and artists. It's a mini-Oscars, done southern style with designer frocks and tuxedos accessorized by huge hair, sparkling sequins, oversized belt buckles, and cowboy hats.

As Taylor was ushered along the red carpet at the back of the Sommet Center, wearing a glitzy floor-length dress that night, she must have felt confident. Nominated in four categories, including best female and the daddy of them all, Entertainer of the Year, was an astonishing achievement—although *Fearless* was the top-selling album of the year in America (with 3.2 million sales), and her tour had sold out in minutes. There weren't too many artists who could match Taylor Swift on sales figures, but would the industry feel she deserved to be honored for the prestigious Entertainer of the Year award just yet? Before of the ceremony Wynona Judd, the daughter half of country duo the Judds, had wondered out loud if Taylor was deserving at this stage in her career and told *USA Today* that the teen's nomination for the prestigious award could be "too much of a good thing too soon."

The CMA Awards are not just the premier trophies for country music's best, they are the gold seal of approval from peers and the country music industry that a newbie has arrived and legitimately deserves to be named the best in class. Established country stars feel oddly protective about the CMA Awards, especially when more pop-sounding acts are in the running to win, or do win. Older stars rebelled when crossover singers like Olivia Newton-John and John Denver were honored by the CMA in the 1970s. More recently the intrinsically conservative Nashville industry took six years to give a certain midriff-baring Canadian a CMA award, having been persuaded by Shania's enormous sales numbers and public opinion to name Twain the Entertainer of the Year in 1999.

Not only was Taylor up for four awards, including the big one, she was opening the show.

AND THE WINNER IS . . .

After a phony interview and comedy skit with TV presenter Nancy O'Dell that ended with Taylor's tongue-in-cheek warning, "If guys don't want me to write bad songs about them, they shouldn't do bad things," Swift opened the 2009 proceedings with a barnstorming version of "Forever and Always." Tossing an armchair away and sliding down a fireman's pole before shaking out all her nervous energy, Swift belted out the song while writhing flat on the ground. This was not the way your parents remembered CMA Awards shows.

Show co-hosts Brad Paisley and Carrie Underwood, hinting perhaps that this would be Taylor's night, wasted no time in bringing up KanyeGate with a quick parody of Willie Nelson's "Mamas Don't Let Your Babies Grow Up to Be Cowboys" reworked to "Mamas, Don't Let Your Babies Grow Up to Be Kanye."

BELOW: An emotional Taylor accepting the award for Entertainer of the Year from Faith Hill and Tim McGraw in 2009.

When Taylor won her Music Video of the Year award, Kanye figured into the proceedings again. After Swift returned to her seat, Carrie Underwood told Paisley that she felt that his video was also great. While he was jokingly thanking the producers, veteran country singer Little Jimmy Dickens appeared on stage, took the microphone, and said: "Excuse me. Excuse me, sir. Excuse me; I'll let you finish later. Now, Brad Paisley, I know you had a nice video and all that, but Taylor Swift had the best video of all time. You go girl!" Taylor roared with laughter.

Taylor continued the Kanye theme when she won Female Vocalist of the Year. After Lee Ann Womack and Kris Kristofferson handed her the award, Taylor said: "I want to thank every single person tonight for not running up on stage during my speech."

Finally, as anticipated, Taylor was presented with the Entertainer of the Year trophy by her old pals Tim McGraw and his superstar wife, Faith Hill. The nineteen-year-old Swift then called her band on stage as the Sommet Center erupted and became, for a minute or two, another Taylor Nation concert scene as teenage fans screamed, howled, and waved "We love you, Taylor" signs. Down in the audience Scott Swift cried.

"I'll never forget this moment because in this moment everything that I have ever wanted has just happened to me," Taylor said as she too felt the occasion overwhelm her and bring her to tears. Taylor Swift was now the youngest ever recipient of the prized Entertainer of the Year award. Only six other female acts had won the esteemed honor, and she was in sparkling and cool company—the Dixie

ABOVE: Taylor performs with her band at *Dick Clark's New Year's Rockin' Eve* with Ryan Seacrest, 2009.

won the esteemed honor, and she was in sparkling and cool company—the Dixie Chicks, Reba McEntire, Dolly Parton, Loretta Lynn, Shania Twain, and Barbara Mandrell. Barbara Mandrell, the only woman to win Entertainer of the Year twice, was at the Sommet Center that night being elected into the Country Music Hall of Fame. Ever gracious, she told the press she was delighted to see Taylor Swift pick up the big one, saying: "I think it will be exciting to see where she takes it because she entertains you."

"I think [what happened] about thirty–seven minutes ago is what stands out for me my whole life," Swift told reporters backstage after her moment of glory. "You guys, I didn't expect to win, so I'm really at a loss for words."

Some of the older country artists like Wynonna Judd and Randy Travis, a country heavyweight who ruled the pre–Garth Brooks roost, were not sure she'd paid her dues enough to be given the prestigious Entertainer of the Year award, though. Travis politely told *People* magazine: "When you look at the body of work that she has written at the age when she came into this business, it's remarkable. It really is. But do I think that entertainer of the year might have been a little early? In my opinion, yes, for whatever that's worth."

But ever the smart one, Swift had a ready answer for her critics: "I feel like it's been fast but it's also been a growth curve. I've watched the CMA Awards for as long as I can remember, and I got to come to my first one when I was 15. I know what it means to win a CMA award. So I look at it from both ways."

Besides, two of the biggest starts in country had her back. "I think she worked her tail off the last couple [of years] and she deserves to win," Faith Hill told *People* magazine. McGraw chipped in, saying: "I've been doing this a long time and she's got a better head on her shoulders than I do, so I don't know how anybody could complain about that."

Brad Paisley, co-host of the evening's celebrations, was also delighted for her: "She has taken the music world by storm," Paisley said. "She's the biggest artist in music right now, by far. It's hands down. She's entertainer of the year in country music, no doubt, and I'm really proud of her."

Of course, Taylor Swift, never one to get carried away by the adrenaline rush of fame and success, kept it all real with a typically Taylor tweet the following morning: "Just wrapped up a cereal party with my mom and dad at the kitchen table. What a night."

MORE, MORE, MORE

The year 2010—surprise, surprise—started with Taylor Swift accomplishing yet another childhood dream. On February 14, a romantic comedy from Hollywood veteran Garry Marshall (*Runaway Bride*, *Pretty Woman*) opened worldwide. The movie, *Valentine's Day*, an ensemble piece with interrelating episodes and characters, was not dissimilar to *Love, Actually*, Taylor Swift's all-time favorite movie. Lining up alongside Hollywood luminaries Julia Roberts, Ashton Kutcher, Jessica Alba, Taylor Lautner, and Jamie Foxx was everyone's favorite teenage singing star, Taylor Swift. In America, *Valentine's Day* debuted with $52.4 million earnings on its opening weekend, grabbing the number 1 box office spot with ease.

Pop stars trying their hand on the silver screen is nothing new, from Madonna back in the 1980s to Beyoncé, Mariah Carey, and Justin Timberlake in the twenty-first century. Even Britney had given it a shot. Most fared poorly, but a few, like Timberlake (most notably in 2010's *The Social Network*), seemed able to transition from one performance medium to another and earn the respect of the critics, despite them being always ready to pooh-pooh any celebrity's attempt to switch careers.

RIGHT: Taylor in a scene from *CSI: Crime Scene Investigation*, her favorite TV show in which she guest-starred in 2009.

In 2008, a remarkably composed Taylor Swift had enjoyed a stint presenting at the VMAs (the year before KanyeGate) and had given fair evidence that she could excel at more than just music performance. Her composed and accomplished presenting performance set some thinking that she might just have what it takes to tackle TV and movies. That a director such as Garry Marshall would not only recognize Taylor's potential but actually write a role into a blockbuster movie especially for her was a significant compliment.

Taylor had just a small part in *Valentine's Day*; she certainly wasn't carrying the film with her name and status, so the chances were good for her to make the transition to big screen quietly and subtly. By then of course Taylor, being Taylor, had already dipped her toes into the acting process on a smaller scale the previous year, with a well-received guest-starring role on the TV crime show *CSI: Las Vegas*.

Because life on the road, even for a bubbly teen like Taylor Swift, can become a tedious endurance test, touring performers look for diversion and entertainment as they travel. After all, America is a vast country, and country stars usually tour more than their pop and rock counterparts. They do so, though, typically in pimped-out buses full of the kind of luxuries that even well-appointed houses might lack.

Taylor loved TV crime shows and watched episodes of *Law and Order* and *CSI* constantly on the state-of-the-art flat–screen TV in her tour bus. Apparently it was the forensic medicine aspect of *CSI* that really fascinated Taylor, and that particular series became must-see viewing, wherever she was. Buried in MySpace blog posts going back to 2006 are throwaway lines about *CSI*, saying that it was a constant in her on-the-road life. Her dream, according to comments she made to MTV, was not just to appear in an episode but play a character that dies. Then, on January 23, 2009, her blog mentioned *CSI* in an altogether different, intriguing context. She was, according to her MySpace page missive, about to guest–star on an episode of her favorite TV show, *CSI*, and that it was something so amazing she'd tell her grandchildren about it.

TURN, TURN, TURN

Taylor had been in Los Angeles staying with Tim McGraw and Faith Hill while filming the episode of *CSI: Las Vegas*. Taylor would play a sixteen-year-old girl who was murdered by her mother. The episode was called "Turn, Turn, Turn." When initially approached to be in the show, Taylor told CBS News, "I'm so excited, because I'm going to freak out and probably cry when I meet all my favorite characters. I'm so excited, and I can't wait."

Taylor's experience in editing her own MySpace videos as well as her intellectual attraction to the whodunnit format meant that *CSI*, with its fast editing, clever camera work, and well-disguised plot twists, appealed to her on several levels. She told MTV, "With *CSI: Las Vegas*, it kind of pairs up all of the things that I'm obsessed with, other than music. When I see really cool editing and really cool effects done, I admire it, and I like to go back and watch it again. I also love the whole crime-scene aspect of it, of figuring things out and analyzing."

Playing against her good-girl image and covering her trademark blond locks, Taylor, with short brown hairstyle, became Haley Jones, a sixteen-year-old living with her parents at a rundown motel, the scene of murder. Swift was in her element. The episode unfolded in a series of flashbacks covering a year in the life of her character, a troubled and defiant teen with a smart mouth who strikes up a friendship with one of the show's detectives. Taylor got to play her death scene when her character's mother stabbed her with a pair of scissors.

Taylor received good reviews for her first acting role. VH1 called her enthusiastic and recommended she pursue more acting roles. The *New York Times* also saw something in her performance, noting the "pleasing flashes of subversion here, a soft launch of her inevitable growing up, and out, of her porcelain persona."

ABOVE: Taylor performs during the Country Thunder music festival in Wisconsin in 2009.

Producers of the show were more than delighted when Swift brought her vast teen audience—the Taylor Nation—to the show. The episode topped the 20 million viewers mark and was beaten in the ratings only by an *American Idol* wildcard special.

Despite TV closing the gap on movies in terms of credibility, status, and glamor (thanks to cable networks like HBO and Showtime and masterful TV movies and series like *The Wire*, *Band of Brothers*, *Dexter*, and *Pacific*), Hollywood movies still remain the pinnacle of any acting career. Taylor Swift, intensely busy with the

Fearless tour in the summer of 2009, hardly needed to detour into a Hollywood movie career, but when she was approached, the romantic nature of the movie was too tempting to let pass by.

"I got a phone call from [film director] Garry Marshall," she told *Trailer Addict*. "Saying, 'Taylor, I want to have lunch or breakfast with you. I really want you to be in this movie. Will you? Will you let me write a part for you?' And I could not believe it. I couldn't believe that, because I didn't have the time to be a big role in this movie, Garry was going to write in a small role for me. It blew my mind."

YOUNG LOVE

Taylor's character, Felicia, is involved in a teen romance with Willy, played by *New Moon* teen heartthrob Taylor Lautner. The innocent, sweet affair has them agreeing to wait until Valentine's Day before consummating their relationship. Lautner gives Swift a white teddy bear that she carries with her everywhere she goes.

Taylor especially enjoyed filming her first movie scenes in a high school. "We're walking in school and it's interesting because we shot this scene in an active high school. Active. As in school was in session while we're filming. Every thirty minutes there would be a bell that would ring and hundreds of students were pouring out, exactly where we were, and there were lots of people screaming out of windows, and groups of kids gathering together chanting things. It was definitely an interesting and very exciting day. For me to step out of my comfort zone and try comedy, and have one of the coolest directors and a legendary director laughing that hard at my first scene, it was really wonderful."

"I want my fans to know I'm just the same girl I was when the first album came out"

Reviews were mixed, mostly focusing on the confusion of Garry Marshall's direction. The *Philadelphia Inquirer*, being nice, however, called it a "pleasant, undemanding movie that takes place over eighteen hours on V-Day." Taylor however, did herself justice, as most reviewers noted.

Taylor was only on screen for around ten minutes but showed enough potential to be singled out by reviewers. CMT.com reviewer Chris Willman wrote: "Swift makes the most of that limited time and is—quite unsurprisingly—a dynamic screen presence whom the camera clearly adores. You might think of her extended cameo as a high-profile, low-pressure screen test for bigger and better roles, and she passes with flying colors."

She also gained something else from the experience: a new beau, Taylor Lautner. Rumors of another celebrity romance started when the two Taylors were spotted together around L.A. while filming the movie.

Taylor very publicly hugged Lautner at her October 9 concert in Rosemont, Illinois. They were then spotted on several dates, often chaperoned by Andrea Swift. While neither star confirmed the rumors, Taylor's sly "Hi, Taylor" aside during her *SNL* monologue did seem to suggest that there was something behind the latest tabloid obsession. Then, as happened with Joe Jonas, it all came out in the media when the two broke up, or at least stopped seeing each other.

At the end of December *Us* magazine reported that it was all over. "It wasn't really developing into anything, and wasn't going to, so they decided they were better as friends. There was no chemistry." The romance died at Taylor's birthday party in Nashville on December 13.

OPPOSITE: As Taylor's fame and popularity around the world grew, so did interest in her love life, as this cover showing the young star with Taylor Lautner shows.

PATSY CLINE

THESE days when people in Nashville talk about "crossover", they are usually talking about a country singer's attempts to broaden their musical horizons and embark on a more pop or rock career. Dolly Parton, Kenny Rogers, Garth Brooks, Shania Twain, and of course Taylor Swift have all combined country with pop to great effect. But it's no easy task and many before have failed, often ending up with a diluted bland music that's neither pop nor country.

Back in the 1950s the idea of a country artist making it big in the mainstream pop market was close to absurd. Only a few managed it in the 1950s and 1960s, but one who did was Patsy Cline. She had to drop the rockabilly tone of her early recordings, though, and cut a song that she thought sounded like "a little old pop song." In spring 1957 Patsy Cline and "Walking after Midnight" entered the hallowed pop charts for the first time. Once she started working with Nashville producer Owen Bradley and his lush string-backed arrangements in the 1960s, she became a true crossover singing star. Proof came in 1961 when "I Fall to Pieces" caught the imagination of the American public, rising to number 1 on the country chart and crossing over to the pop chart at number 12. That year she was badly hurt in a car accident, but recovered enough to enjoy hits with "Crazy" and "She's Got You," both of which scored well on both country and pop charts.

Cline, born Virginia Patterson Hensley in Virginia, was very much a country girl and insisted on recording songs by country writers like Hank Cochran, Harlan Howard, and Willie Nelson (who gave Cline her best-known song, "Crazy"). Producer Bradley, however, envisioned her as diva pop singer, and when both approaches combined on great material, the so-called Nashville sound of strings and vocal choirs took country music into the pop realm for the first time on a major scale. (The legendary Chet Atkins was doing a similar thing with Jim Reeves around the same time.)

Cline had a great reputation among her peers. She stood up for women at a time when female singers had very little power, especially in traditional and conservative Nashville. She could also raise hell with the best of them and was a regular drinker at Tootsie's Orchid Lounge, where she was known to sit and tell a racy joke or two over several beers. Cline broke down countless doors in the music business. She was the first woman to play New York's upmarket Carnegie Hall and to headline her own concert in Las Vegas. But Patsy was also one of the girls and took the young Loretta Lynn under her wing to such effect that now Loretta Lynn remembers her as "my closest friend, my protector, my inspiration."

Tragically, Patsy Cline was killed in a plane crash in Camden, Tennessee, in 1963. She was on her way home from a gig in Kansas City. Singers Hawkshaw Hawkins and Cowboy Copas also died in the crash. But so strong was Cline's voice and personality that her career never really ended.

She had a number of posthumous hits as her record company, Decca, continued to release tracks to radio. In 1967 her *12 Greatest Hits* album was released and was the top-selling hits collection by a female country artist for years to follow. Patsy Cline was inducted into the Country Music Hall of Fame in 1973, the first female solo artist to be elected to that honor.

In 1984 Jessica Lange played Patsy in a movie biopic, *Sweet Dreams*, bringing a new generation to Cline's brand of country music. In 1995 Cline was given a Grammy Lifetime Achievement Award. A few years later she received an honor that not many from Nashville have been given, a posthumous star on the Hollywood Walk of Fame.

There's so much in Patsy's voice and her life to inspire a young female country singer that it's unsurprising that Taylor Swift is a fan. So, if she occasionally gets criticism from folks in Nashville for her pop sound and not playing pure traditional country, Taylor can console herself with the fact that Patsy Cline is now revered and honored as a country music legend, despite being accused of much the same thing in the 1960s.

OPPOSITE: Influential country star Patsy Cline in her heyday in the 1960s.

8

Better than Revenge

WORD on the street had it that Taylor Swift walked away from her never clearly defined relationship with Taylor Lautner showing none of the hurt or thirst for payback that had colored previous breakups. The year ended with plenty of celebrations and parties courtesy of the holiday season. Despite the breakup, Taylor had plenty to be happy about as 2009 rolled to a close. She was the bestselling artist in America, and before she'd celebrated her twentieth birthday she had received country music's most coveted Entertainer of the Year award.

As 2010 began the engines started up again on the Taylor Swift express, promising more highs than she'd ever imagined—although the year would also see a setback or two to test her inner strength, resilience, and character. Inevitably perhaps, a Taylor Swift backlash started to rumble in the background as her success continued to grow. Nashville is small town, particularly within the music business part of it. Like any city of dreams it tends to foster rival cliques, usually defined by those who find success and those who fail and continue to struggle, in doing so sometimes becoming envious and bitter toward those who make it to the worldwide stage.

And that doesn't just apply to artists; the jealousy and resentment toward those who've found success filters through music publishing companies, record labels, radio and TV stations, Web sites, PR companies, catering companies, and booking agents. All aspects of the business, to some extent, become tinged with bitterness when success proves elusive. At Nashville's numerous industry events and in bars, restaurants, meat-and-threes, and coffee shops, artists and their representatives who had toiled many a year to achieve a fraction of what Taylor managed in two years were attributing her success to anything but talent. She was just a novelty, they whispered, she was taking advantage of the Internet, she couldn't even sing, she was a puppet who didn't really write her own songs, and her wealthy father bought her all the success she had enjoyed.

Of course none of these gripes was true. They'd said much the same about Garth Brooks twenty years before. In Garth's case he had succeeded, the cynics said, because he was a marketing genius—forgetting, of course, that even the most sophisticated marketing campaign cannot create onstage charisma or write songs that people will relate to, memorize, and sing back at the artist in stadiums from London to Buenos Aires. Back in the 1990s, the anti-Shania brigade claimed she couldn't carry a tune and that she was merely a puppet in the hands of her husband, Def Leppard producer Mutt Lange. What they forgot (or ignored) was that Shania's pre-Mutt debut album was low key but high in musical quality, and anyone who'd seen her sing at early showcases knew that she could carry a tune with the best of them.

The Taylor haters had their opportunity to express their resentment-fueled views when the Grammy nominations were announced in December 2009. Taylor and her mother were sitting in their L.A. hotel room editing Taylor's home video when word came of her astonishing eight nominations for the 2010 Grammy Awards. Beyoncé received two more nominations, but incredibly, Taylor was three ahead of the latest global pop sensation, Lady Gaga. "To be recognized by the Grammys is the ultimate honor, and all I know is that when I write about this in my journal tonight it will be in all capital letters and underlined four times, and there will be lots of exclamation points in this entry because I never imagined I'd get to write this kind of journal entry," Swift told the Associated Press.

PREVIOUS PAGE: Taylor headlining at the Bayou Country Superfest on May 29, 2010 in Baton Rouge.

OPPOSITE: Taylor is called to the stage to collect an award at the Grammys, 2010.

BACKLASH

The Taylor Swift critics in Nashville could barely contain themselves. She may have duped the CMA, who had been pressured by the public into making her Entertainer of the Year, they said, but there was no way the Grammy voters were going to fall for the same tricks. Sure, she was nominated as the inevitable by-product of her commercial success, but the Grammys knew better than to take her seriously enough to give her an award, went the anti-Taylor rants. No way was she deserving of pop music's most valued award and honor. Was she?

What the small-minded and bitter naysayers in Nashville forgot, though, was that Taylor Swift was no longer just a country artist. She had transcended the small town mind-set of some on Music Row and was already a world-famous music star, whose achievements were being monitored, analyzed, admired, and respected by the global record industry. So it was that on January 31 the Staples Center in Los Angeles would prove to be the big test. Maybe she'd pick up one of the three country nominations she was up for, but Album of the Year, the most valued and coveted Grammy? Surely not. But then "surely not" was hardly an appropriate phrase for Taylor Swift's astonishing music career.

"To be recognized by the Grammys is the ultimate honor."

In any other year than this, her "backlash year," headlines would have focused on how Taylor Swift came and conquered, picking up three country music awards for Best Female Country Vocal Performance, Best Country Song for "White Horse," and Best Country Album for *Fearless*. And that she then stunned the Grammy audience by beating pop heavyweights Beyoncé, Dave Matthews, Lady Gaga, and the Black Eyed Peas for the big one, Album of the Year.

Taylor loved her moment of glory. "This is the story that all of us, when we're eighty years old and we are telling the same stories over and over again to our grandkids and they're so annoyed with us . . . this is the story that we're going to be telling over and over again—in 2010, that we got to win Album of the Year at the Grammys! Thank you, thank you, thank you!"

And that should have been it, a truly incredible accomplishment for one so young (the youngest ever to manage such a feat) and a perfect start to the year. But it was Taylor's performance that grabbed the headlines the next day. She took the stage to sing a medley of "Today Was a Fairytale" and "You Belong with Me," plus a duet with legendary singer Stevie Nicks, who joined her onstage for a version of the Fleetwood Mac classic "Rhiannon." It wasn't Taylor's best performance, and there were a few wayward notes, which gave the critics the excuse to launch into her with venom.

OPPOSITE: Taylor won an amazing four awards at the 2009 Grammy Awards.

The Washington Post said: "To borrow a phrase from Montgomery Burns, it was more 'off-key caterwauling.'" EW.com sniped: "There's no doubt that someone was badly off-key . . . I'm afraid my money's on Taylor." The *Los Angeles Times* joined in with, "Swift gave a strikingly bad vocal performance at Staples Center on Sunday, sounding tinny and rhythmically flat-footed as she shared the microphone with the distinctive Stevie Nicks."

Attack Taylor Swift and you attack Scott Borchetta, and the battle-hardened record company executive wasn't about to sit and watch his twenty-year-old artist be slammed in the press without standing up for her and offering some thoughts and explanations: "We had a volume problem in the ear. So, she was concerned that she wasn't able to hear everything in the mix," Borchetta said. "That's just part of live TV . . . So you're going to have difficulties on occasion. Unfortunately, on one of the biggest stages, we did have a technical issue. She couldn't hear herself like she had in rehearsal.

"The facts say she is the undisputed best communicator that we've got," he said. "So when she says something or feels something it affects more people than anybody else. Maybe she's not the best technical singer, but she is the best emotional

singer. Everybody gets up there and is technically perfect people don't seem to want more of it. There's not an artist in any other format that people want more of than they want of Taylor. I think [the critics] are missing the whole voice of a generation that is happening right in front of them. Maybe they are jealous or can't understand that. But obviously the people that she talks to are engaged with her. No one is perfect on any given day. Maybe in that moment we didn't have the best night, but in the same breath, maybe we did."

Taylor's hometown newspaper, the *Tennessean*, a periodical that knows a little bit about the musical arts, jumped into Taylor's corner. Pete Cooper, senior music contributor, wrote: "Swift chose not to have her voice tuned at the Grammys, and then she delivered a less than convincing performance that came on the heels of other less than convincing awards show performances. Is she a particularly strong singer? Of course not. Is she a talentless fraud? Of course not. She makes records using the same technology and methodology as everyone else in town. She's a twenty-year-old who got famous before coming into her own as a vocalist. Give her some time."

TINA TURNER

WHEN Taylor Swift was interviewed in the early days of her career she often dropped the name Tina Turner into the conversation when asked about her musical influences. It showed that even as a youngster, Taylor was able to see beyond the contemporary music scene, grasp the bigger picture, and identify with one of rock'n'roll's most significant performers. Tina Turner rose from poverty, became a global star with Ike Turner, fought against domestic violence, and emerged as one of the world's top solo acts in the last twenty–five years of the twentieth century. *Rolling Stone* has called her one of the greatest singers of all time, and she's sold an estimated 180 million records during her long career.

Anna Mae Bullock, as she was known, (the name Tina Turner came later), was raised in Nutbush, Tennessee, and when she turned eighteen headed to St. Louis to try her luck as a singer. Hanging out in music clubs she became a fan of rock'n'roll guitarist and influential Sun Records (where Elvis Presley began his career) A&R man Ike Turner. Tina smartly figured a good first step in her career would be to persuade Ike to let her sing. He liked what he heard, and when his regular vocalist failed to show up for a recording session one day in 1960, Anna Mae sang "A Fool in Love." The song was a hit and a new star was born. Ike named her Tina Tuner, they married in Tijuana, and the new Ike and Tina Turner Revue became international stars with hits like "It's Gonna Work Out Fine" and the Phil Spector–produced "River Deep, Mountain High."

The hits continued through the 1970s, notably "Proud Mary" and Tina's self-penned "Nutbush City Limits," but behind the scenes all was not well. As Tina would later describe in her autobiography, Ike Turner was abusive, and their marriage ended when Tina fled right before a concert in Dallas, with barely a dollar in her pocket but determined to start over, on her own. With kids to support she played small clubs and worked as a housekeeper to keep food on her family's table during some lean times.

Feeling that L.A. would never accept her, she moved to Europe, where Ike and Tina had a huge fan base, and lived in several European cities. When Capitol Records considered dropping her, David Bowie's support pushed them to reconsider, and she worked on a comeback album, the career-defining *Private Dancer* album of 1984. The record put her back on top with the hits "Private Dancer," "Better Be Good to Me," and "What's Love Got to Do with It," winning her two American Music Awards and four Grammys in the process.

From that point on Tina Turner's career was unstoppable. She became a movie star in *Mad Max beyond Thunderdome* and one of the biggest live performance acts in the world. On her South American tour in 1987, she played to 182,000 people in the Maracana Arena in Rio de Janeiro, the largest audience ever assembled for a single performer.

The 1993 movie *What's Love Got to Do with It*, based on her no-holds-barred autobiography *I, Tina*, told the world about her life and struggles with husband Ike. It wasn't a pretty Hollywood movie, and Turner's comeback seemed all the more remarkable given the obstacles she'd been forced had to overcome.

She broke more live performance records in 1997, when her world tour broke ticket sales records and grossed more than $130 million. After semi-retiring in the late 1990s, Tina Turner came back to music in 2008, for a fiftieth anniversary tour, one of the most successful tours of the year.

In 2002 the state of Tennessee honored Tina Turner by renaming State Route 19 Tina Turner Highway as a "lasting tribute to this native daughter of Nutbush, Tennessee, who has continued the exceptional musical legacy of this state as an artist and entertainer of singular stature."

If Taylor Swift continues to write, sing, perform, and record for the next forty-something years like Tina, then there will probably be not just a road in her native state of Pennsylvania, but an interstate freeway or two named after her.

OPPOSITE: Tina Turner at the height of her success in 1984.

FIGHT BACK

As the news of Taylor's public flogging spread, some of Nashville's most respected names defended her. Naomi Judd wrote to the editor of the *Tennessean* newspaper:

> Remember the puzzles, "What's wrong with this picture?" You search for faults, ignoring the overall larger picture. Reference Taylor Swift. Multi-talented, she not only sings well enough to strike a chord with a huge audience, Taylor single-handedly introduced country music to a much-welcomed younger demographic and generated international interest. She writes, dances, acts and is a dazzling performer. Taylor is the best-dressed young female artist today, in league with Hollywood's most glamorous stars. When I met her I was impressed by her sincere transparent niceness. Taylor's a lovely young lady.
>
> Having sung many times at the Grammys, I can tell you that the stress and anxiety of performing in front of the world's top artists in every genre of music is tortuous for even the most seasoned singer.
>
> Smarts, manners, and class. Why can't fault-finders see that she is a sorely needed role model? We're aware of how lyrics and musicians can influence our society. If America ever needed positive role models, it's now.
>
> If there's an award for being the best role model for her generation, I'd like to be the one to give it to Taylor Swift.

Nashville legend Charlie Daniels ("Devil Went Down to Georgia") offered his support in an interview with *Country Weekly* magazine:

> I hear people criticize her and I think, "C'mon, leave her alone." They say she can't sing, well she can sing. Bob Dylan couldn't sing. Leonard Cohen couldn't sing. I mean, they can certainly sing in their own way, but you

BELOW AND OPPOSITE: Taylor's image and interview reaches the UK in the *Sunday Times Style* magazine, February 2010.

The night before I interview the country-music megastar Taylor Swift in LA, I see her play at a charity fundraiser in Beverly Hills. The hot scent of lilies fills the room, which is heaving with diamonds, tumbling blonde curls, facelifts and fur. The chatter, above the clink of champagne glasses, is all about Taylor, who smiles as the flashbulbs pop around her like the brightest shower of stars. During dinner, the host, Tom Hanks, eulogises about Taylor's "unbelievable poise and talent." There's an auction and someone pays $50,000 for a signed guitar.

Before dinner, I am introduced to Taylor, who jumps up from her place beside Steven Spielberg to hug me. She's incredibly charming ("Oh, hi! I love your dress! You look so cute! What perfume are you wearing? I love it"), and in a room full of extreme facial reconstruction, there's something endearing about her slightly skewy face, which is pretty, but also looks real. When she sings, Reese Witherspoon has to restrain her daughter, Ava, from storming the stage. Taylor's stagecraft is impeccable, both intimate and big-scale, and she uses her international hair to full effect. "Thank you soooo much. It's an honour to be here. Wow!" she murmurs, sounding genuinely surprised at the raucous standing ovation.

"Isn't she delicious?" says a woman in diamonds beside me. "She's what America needs right now. So sweet." Yes, I think, very sweet. But does sweetness make a great country singer?

Until last week, the only thing I could have told you about Taylor Swift was that Kanye West stormed the stage in protest when she won at the MTV Music Awards. I couldn't name her songs, but in HMV an assistant, with tattoos running up both arms and a faceful of metal, had given her his thumbs up. "We stock her under country, as well as rock and pop. She's my guilty pleasure," he said, surprising me, as I didn't have him down as country-music fan. Waiting to interview her, I realise there's much about the dizzying rise of 20-year-old Taylor that's surprising. She's the top digital-selling artist ever, and her second album, Fearless, went double platinum in four weeks. Last year, every single tour date sold out within minutes. She vies with Mariah Carey and the Beatles for the most top 20 Billboard chart debuts, and she has 5m Facebook friends. Crossover? You betcha.

For a long time, country music has been taboo, lampooned as redneck music that berates you to stand by your man, even when that man is a tobacco-chewing addict who can't say I love you. In the 1980s, country gained a reputation as a dodgy genre saddled to a sweaty, overweight, balding man with a terrible taste in shirts — Garth Brooks. Line dancing and Billy Ray Cyrus didn't help, either. Lesbians liked country, but nobody else did.

I should know. I'm not a lesbian, but I've always loved country music. On the school bus, my contemporaries wore stonewashed jeans and fluoro socks, with Bros, Frankie Goes to Hollywood and Wham! on their Walkmans. I liked gingham shirts, Tammy Wynette, Willie Nelson and Steve Earle, and they thought I was a complete weirdo. I didn't care because, this being country, it made it all the sweeter. Country has accompanied every love affair I've ever had, and it's also changed the course of my life. The wild energy of Willie Nelson was the reason I moved, aged 22, to Texas, to ▶▶

AMERICA'S SWEETHEART

TAYLOR SWIFT IS A MUSIC PHENOMENON – HER SUGAR-COATED
STYLE A PERFECT ANTIDOTE TO HER NATION'S ILLS.
CLOVER STROUD, WHO GREW UP LISTENING TO COUNTRY, ASKS
HER IF SHE THINKS SHE WILL BE ONE OF THE GREATS

PHOTOGRAPHS *RAYMOND MEIER*

Dolly girl: Taylor Swift is country music's latest crossover queen couldn't compare them to [Italian tenor] Enrico Caruso. But they left us some of the greatest songs we'll ever have. Taylor Swift is a great little writer, kind of reminiscent of a folk writer in a way, trying to document what's going on in her life from her point of view.

She is a very very decent young woman who is a much better role model than some of these that are held up to admiration. She's always been very down to earth and very humble. I like people who can handle a certain degree of stardom without taking themselves too seriously.

Despite the criticism, Taylor continued writing and embarked on the Australian dates of the Fearless tour. She was also thrilled to be selected as the new face of Covergirl. In March, representatives from the National Academy of Recording Arts and Sciences (NARAS; the Grammy organizers) flew to Nashville for a private dinner with Big Machine Records and representatives from the American Music Awards, the Country Music Association, and the Academy of Country Music. The reason was that *Fearless* had been officially recognized as the most awarded album in the history of country music. NARAS still had a few more industry milestones to honor Taylor with. She now had more than thirteen million total record sales and more than twenty–five million digital downloads. They also gave Taylor her six-time platinum certificate for *Fearless*.

The dinner gave Scott Borchetta an opportunity to put some perspective on Taylor's whirlwind ride to the top: "We tend to always look forward when it comes to Taylor, but tonight it was time to stop for a moment and look back on one of the most successful music works of all time," he said. "The eighteen months of our lives known as the *Fearless* era have been history-making, euphoric, and triumphant. The sales, the airplay, the accolades, and the awards have all just been incredible. But, most important to me is that my friend Taylor and her collective team of family, record label, management, and her road family continue to raise the bar with work ethic, achievement and enjoyment. Dreams do come true."

▶▶ find out if those pick-up-truck-driving, honky-tonk-dancing cowboys were for real. They were, so I got a job as a cowgirl on a ranch. Before I left, I got "Texas" tattooed on my left biceps on the way to ride a bucking horse in a rodeo with a cowboy called Jimmy Joe. Country music is the reason why, nine years later, I'm mother to a son called Jimmy Joe and a daughter called Dolly. No need to explain her name. It's certainly part of the reason I married a hard-drinking musician. It spoke to me, too, when I stood in the wreckage of that marriage, giving my life a narrative I understood that helped me step out of it.

I'm not the only woman with a tangible connection to country music. It had a huge impact on housewives in small town America in the 1950s and 1960s, when Patsy Cline, Kitty Wells and Loretta Lynn gave them a voice of their own, even if it was one singing about Fist City and Don't Come Home a' Drinkin' (With Lovin' on Your Mind).

So where does Taylor fit into this? Her life, by her own admission, is "an insane fairy tale that sometimes feels like a movie". There's a lot of romance to the story of 10-year-old Taylor singing her socks off at every country show that passed through her home town in Pennsylvania. You also have to hand it to her for posting demo tapes through the letter box of every record producer in Nashville when she was 11, and having the self-belief to keep on singing when she was rejected by them all. Her parents, Scott, a stockbroker, and Andrea, a housewife, moved Taylor and her brother, Austin, to Nashville when she was 14. A smart move, as Taylor, who writes all her songs, was spotted singing at the famous Bluebird Cafe, her co-star in a forthcoming movie, Valentine's Day. I'm worrying, too, youngest person ever to have signed a songwriting deal with Sony/ATV Publishing. A recording deal followed, and since then she's made music history.

Moments before we meet, her publicist tells me I mustn't ask her about relationships, which seems surprising for someone whose multi-million-pound industry revolves around singing about nothing but relationships. She has been linked to the musician John Mayer and Twilight's Taylor Lautner, her co-star in a forthcoming movie, Valentine's Day. I'm worrying, too, about how this cult of a girl can really sing country, when country, at its best, is about suffering and soul, and the seductive and seedy underbelly of domestic life. As Tammy Wynette, country's high priestess of pain, said: "The sad part about a happy ending is that there's nothing to write about." Taylor's songs are about crushes in 10th grade and high-school love, but where does that leave the big themes of country music: infidelity, alcoholism, domestic violence and God? The biggest tragedy I can find in Taylor's lovely life is her claim that she was dumped by Joe Jonas, who wears a chastity ring.

I have to hand it to her parents: they've drummed impeccable Southern manners into her. She has super-model limbs, curly hair pulled back and eyelids sagging under fake lashes, the only artifice in an otherwise girlish look. She is wearing a bright blue dress with a belted yellow top, and a huge key around her neck. "A gift from a friend, who found it at Wembley. Singing there means so much to me, and I thought it appropriate to wear it today," she says.

Answers roll out of her mouth with polish and spontaneity. She tells me about the "whimsical" (a word she uses often) pleasures of growing up surrounded by animals on a Christmas-tree farm, and paints such an adorable picture of herself running through the fields "like a crazy kid with tangled hair", it could have been created by Walt Disney. She's deeply grateful to her parents, of course. "They never pushed me. Getting into music was my ambition, but when they realised that's what I wanted, they drove me to guitar lessons and helped me figure out which amps I needed. They gave me this wonderful space to be imaginative and to dream."

She tells me about the apartment she has bought in Nashville, where she's having a giant birdcage installed in which to play music, and how she loves making spiced pumpkin cookies with frosted icing. Sometimes she veers into beauty-queen speak, rolling off pat answers about the importance of following a dream, and telling me that "if I had one wish, it would be the power to heal". But she seems emotionally articulate as well, which she puts down to having spent so long talking about herself in interviews. "You get to know yourself pretty well. It's like therapy," she says, laughing.

I'M FASCINATED BY LOVE, BECAUSE IT'S SOMETHING YOU CAN NEVER FIGURE OUT. ALL MY MUSIC IS BASED ON PERSONAL EXPERIENCES

Pressed on the subject of boys, she's a little coy. Being on stage gives her a confidence she doesn't have in normal life, she claims. She won't go into details, but doesn't have a bad word to say about Jonas, although she's endlessly forthcoming on the theory, at least, of love. "I'm fascinated by love, because it's something you can never figure out. All my music is based on real personal experiences," she says, quick to point out that "this doesn't mean I've had a lot of boyfriends. One relationship might inspire a whole album. I understand unrequited love, when you've never had a chance to wrap your arms round someone and feel it".

Although she has never experienced "big love", she's holding out for it. "I think there are different levels of compatibility in relationships, and many people find a partial match. Once in a while two people find the perfect match, and we're all envious."

It's hard not to fall for Taylor. The lady in the diamonds was right: she's what America needs right now, a tall glass of cherry soda, a small town girl singing songs about love that we can all relate to. It's not her fault she hasn't suffered, that there isn't a hint of white trash about her. A decade ago, Britney urged us to "hit me baby one more time", a sentiment that coming from Taylor's mouth would sound totally inappropriate — and totally inappropriate, too, for our post-bling, post-gangsta-rap, post-financial-meltdown sensibilities. Taylor has got heart, and represents what's good about the tattered American dream, the pretty girl living the fairy tale who dialodges our jaded cynicism with life.

I hope Taylor's life stays as sweet as she makes it seem today. I hope she never does sing about divorce and tragedy, about the kind of domestic suffering her country-music predecessors went through. I wish her only happiness. But if you were to ask me whether, a decade down the line, she will be singing the kind of songs that change women's lives, the kind of songs Tammy and Kitty and Patsy sang, I would have to say, I doubt it. ◆

"I love it when people call me a role model."

WHEN IT RAINS . . .

In Nashville, Tennessee, on May 1, 2010, it started raining, heavily at first, and then heavy turned torrential as the skies opened. It rained and rained for several days straight, and Tennessee saw its worst flood in history. The damage was shocking, as water rapidly rose as high as roofs across the state. Cars were flooded and left ruined. Thirty people died and thousands were left homeless and desperate. The

historic Grand Ole Opry was almost destroyed as floodwater rose around the hallowed stage. A musicians' storage unit downtown, climate controlled for musical instruments, was flooded and millions of dollars' worth of guitars and music equipment was damaged beyond rescue. Keith Urban lost his guitars, while avid collector and country icon Vince Gill lost thousands of dollars' worth of instruments. Rock star Peter Frampton lost millions of dollars' worth of guitars. Tennessee was in a state of emergency, but it's not known as the Volunteer State for nothing, and neighbors and welfare organizations took to the streets to help the victims. Local TV station WSMV Channel 4 immediately organized a telethon.

"Keep Nashville in your thoughts and prayers."

The show was hosted by Vince Gill, who dipped his hand into his pocket and donated a sizable sum of money. Keith Urban came by the studio and performed. And then Gill announced that Taylor Swift had given a whopping $500,000. "It was the craziest thing that I've ever seen," Taylor said. "I was at my house in Hendersonville; we were staring out the window, thinking it didn't seem like rain. It just seemed like something in a movie. It was really emotional for me because those are the streets I learned to drive on. People's houses are just ruined. It was so heartbreaking to see that in my town, the place that I call home, and the place that I feel most safe. I just send my love to my friends and neighbors who got hit harder than I did."

Later that week Taylor flew to New York for the Met Gala and *Time* magazine's 100 Most Influential People event. Swift wasn't sure how influential she could be, but she certainly gave it all she had by talking up the flood and the issues facing those in Nashville affected by the disaster to any members of the press or media she could. She played ambassador for those who needed help and paused during her concert at the Lincoln Center stage, saying: "We all live in Nashville, Tennessee, and before we play our last song, I would just love it if I could give a shout-out in a room where we have the most influential people in the world. Nashville just had the worst storm that we've ever had in the history of the city, and the Grand Ole Opry is underwater. So, if you could please keep Nashville in your thoughts and prayers that would be wonderful. I would really appreciate it!"

Critics could take a pop at Taylor Swift, but Nashville would never forget what she did for the people of Tennessee during the dark days of the Nashville flood in May 2010.

ARE YOU EXPERIENCED?

With all she'd been though in a crazy two-year period, Taylor Swift was no longer a wide-eyed innocent, writing love notes about boys at Hendersonville High School. She had grown up, mostly in the public eye, and shared most of her growing pains in publicly aired songs and blogs. She told MTV's *The Seven*: "I'm very conscious of the path that I chose in life and that it is a different path than what my friends chose. College and living in a dorm, that would have been my life, if music hadn't been my life. I always keep one eye on that path. I go and I visit my brother at college and I visit my best friend Abigail at college and I attend her journalism class. I have no regrets about the path that I took, but I still try to experience as much as I possibly can in life. Loving this is a big part of my life and sometimes, if you get too tired or you're jetlagged, you might forget. But I always remind myself that I love this."

Radio presenter Shannon McCombs, who had been around Taylor more than most, was aware that the singer was changing: "I think the biggest changes in Taylor were, for the most part, ones you can see in photos. Clothes, professional hair, and makeup. Those are the obvious ones, but those types of changes create confidence as well. She's smart and confident, not cocky. I think she carries herself like a star, and I mean that as a compliment. We've all literally watched her grow into an elegant young lady."

"I'm very conscious of the path that I chose in life."

More importantly, despite the ups and downs (with more ups than downs, to be sure) of dealing with fame and success and living in the celebrity spotlight, Taylor has stayed true to herself and not lost the joy and enthusiasm that shone so brightly in the early days. Some days she was still the eleven-year-old dropping off demo tapes on Sixteenth Avenue. Shannon McCombs recalls: "I was working with Dolly Parton one night at the Opry, and just as we were finishing up, Taylor came into the room overly excited to get to meet Dolly. It was fabulous to watch, because she wasn't trying to act cool or cover her excitement in any way. She was genuinely on a cloud. Just don't see that very often in this business."

As 2010 wore on, Taylor Swift set to work finishing her new album. Despite the incredible demands on her time, Taylor had decided to write all the material for the new release herself. It was partly her way of handling all that had happened. As she told the *Wall Street Journal*, "You have people come into your life shockingly and surprisingly. You have losses that you never thought you'd experience. You have rejection and you have to learn how to deal with that and how to get up the next day and go on with it." Writing songs about such stuff was important to her, and often there was no chance to work with another writer, even if she'd wanted to. "It originally was inspired by circumstance. I would get inspired to write a song at three–thirty in the morning. There's no co-writer around."

GARTH BROOKS

IN Nashville they divide country music into pre–Garth Brooks and post–Garth Brooks eras. That's the phenomenal influence the cowboy singer from Oklahoma has had on country music since the 1990s. A smart operator who managed his career better than most, Brooks had an uncanny ability to sync with the common man right from the beginning. He understands his fans and relates to them as nobody before him, it seems. That was a lesson Taylor Swift took to heart as she remarked when winning a CMT Award in 2009, "I want to thank Garth Brooks for always putting his fans first." Only Swift has since come close to building such a personal and loyal relationship with the fans.

Garth Brooks is the fastest-selling solo artist in music history. His debut album was crammed with fresh, vibrant songwriting and a new, contemporary country sound. His self-titled debut album contained some of his best material: "Much Too Young (To Feel This Damn Old)," "If Tomorrow Never Comes," "Not Counting You," and "The Dance." It quickly became the biggest-selling country album of the 1980s.

Garth's second LP, 1990's *No Fences*, won Album of the Year from the CMA and contained four number 1 hits: "Friends in Low Places," "Unanswered Prayers," "Two of a Kind (Working on a Full House)," and "The Thunder Rolls." The last number, written by Brooks and Pat Alger, was more than a dramatic country epic. It dealt with the previously taboo subject of domestic violence. When it came time to shoot the video, Brooks chose to play the part of the philandering, abusive husband. When the video was banned by CMT (country music's answer to MTV) it became a national talking point. Soon VH1, which rarely played anything country, added the track to its playlist. "Thunder Rolls" won the CMA video of the year award. That established Brooks as an artist with social conscience who was prepared to take risks and take a stand on an issue. And as with most records that get banned or censored, the publicity was priceless. Brooks was known to the all-important rock'n'roll audience.

In 1991 the drinkers' anthem "Friends in Low Places" easily won Single of the Year from both the CMA and ACM, and he won the prestigious CMA Entertainer of the Year award the same year. *Billboard* named him Top Pop and Country Artist, Top Country Album Artist, and Top Country Singles Artist.

How do you follow that? Nobody knew, since Brooks was making history and breaking records as he went. His next album, *Ropin' the Wind*, was the first album ever to debut simultaneously at number 1 on *Billboard*'s Top 200 and country albums charts.

Garth's eagerly awaited 1994 world tour was an unprecedented success, selling out stadiums around the globe. Brooks drew the largest crowd ever to attend a concert in New York's Central Park, and the resulting HBO special, *Garth Live from Central Park*, was the highest-rated original program on the station in 1997.

As a star with great magnetic charisma, he opened countless doors for his Nashville cohorts, establishing new markets overseas and smashing preconceived stereotypes about country artists with several outrageously funny, self-mocking TV appearances on *Saturday Night Live*. Remarkably, a chunky, moderately handsome singer from Oklahoma had made country music hip and brought in a new generation of fans.

Brooks stopped touring at the end of the 1990s, in order to spend time raising his kids. He was able to pick and chooses his moments in the limelight, playing a regular Vegas series of shows and making occasional benefit appearances for causes he believes in. He had not played Nashville in twelve years when he announced a Nashville flood benefit concert in December 2010. Tickets sold out in minutes and demand was such that the one-night show turned into nine concerts over six days, raising a cool $10 million in the process. Taylor got to watch Brooks in action at close quarters during those gigs, and contributed to the cause herself so emphatically. She and Garth showed that true artists have true hearts.

The astute Swift noticed something very significant about Garth Brooks's rise to the top. Aside from creating good music and working as hard as possible, he has given much of himself to his fans. In true Garth style (who famously spent twenty–four hours in line signing autographs at Fan Fair in the 1990s) Taylor Swift gave her fans something special at Fan Fair in June 2010, when she set up a special meet-and-greet session that lasted for more than fifteen hours. Garth Brooks would definitely approve.

OPPOSITE: Garth Brooks in his trademark look of jeans and Stetson.

9

Speak Now

TAYLOR Swift was on a plane traveling to Japan on August 5, 2010, when she discovered that the carefully planned release of her new material was not going to be as smooth as hoped for. The new album was scheduled for an October release with a first single to come out at the end of August.

"When I got on that plane," Taylor told *Entertainment Weekly*, "I just thought I was going to Japan, and I thought it was going to be a regular flight—watch a few movies, take a nap. But an hour into the flight, one of my managers came up to me and said, 'Hey, so, try not to panic. But how would you feel about a release of the single on August 5? So that's 8/5. And eight plus five is thirteen, which is your lucky number!' I said, 'It leaked, didn't it?' And she said, 'Yes.'"

The song was "Mine," and somehow an unofficial and low-quality MP3 file of the recording had popped up online. Such was the hysterical fan demand to hear Taylor's new music that Big Machine opted to give the song an early release to country radio and iTunes to ensure that the correct, finished, and Taylor-approved version would be the one most fans would hear.

A few hours after Taylor received the tip-off on that flight to Japan, "Mine" was in the Top 35 of *Billboard*'s country chart. The album, *Speak Now*, was released on October 25 and entered the *Billboard* 200, selling an astounding 1,047,000 copies, according to Nielsen SoundScan. Nobody had sold that many records in one week since 50 Cent's *The Massacre* back in pre-recession 2005.

Taylor had already given notice that the songs on *Speak Now* would continue to be based on real events when she spoke with *Entertainment Weekly* ahead of the record's release. "I think that whatever I go through in life will be directly reflected in my music. If I have a bunch of different experiences with a bunch of different people and some of them are good and some of them are bad and some of them are confusing, you have an album like this. I like to feel like I've covered every emotion that I've felt in the last two years."

"I'm just making a new record about the last two years of my life."

Critics loved the album. *USA Today* began their review with gushing praise: "What do you do when your star soars so high that fans expect the moon, while critics call you overrated and overexposed? If you're smart, and Taylor Swift is certainly that, you remind everyone what all the fuss was about in the first place. In Swift's case, that's her songwriting. The twenty-year-old phenom crafted the fourteen tracks on *Speak Now* by herself, and like the tunes on 2008's *Fearless*, they're at once precocious and candidly, refreshingly youthful in their perspective."

Paste magazine noted Taylor Swift's growth as an artist: "Swift is growing up, and her lyrics are too. At its best, her songwriting stands as a shining example of Top 40 music—full of cinematic build-ups and addictive repeatability."

In Europe, the *Guardian* called *Speak Now* a "triumph": "At times the self-consciousness of an artist forcing herself into new modes shows—but mostly, *Speak Now* is a triumph. Mine reprises the joyous rush of Swift's breakthrough hit, "Love Story," but depicts love as an adult process rather than a teenage dream. The hazy

crush of "Enchanted" showcases Swift's instinct for capturing emotion with astonishing exactitude—right down to the dread sneaking in at the song's close."

Previewing the song "Innocent" at the 2010 MTV Video Music Awards just twelve months after KanyeGate, Taylor sang the song's conciliatory lyrics after images from the previous year's event flashed on screen. *Speak Now* was definitely going to follow the model of her previous albums and continue with the diary-style songwriting. But if Kanye was getting the Taylor treatment, then he got off lightly.

WHO DO YOU LOVE?

It was *Speak Now*'s apparent confessions from Taylor's personal life that really got the press and media worked up. Naturally enough, bloggers and fans began to pick the album apart for clues and scoops on Taylor's love life, looking for those confessional songs about her love life that made *Fearless* such a revelation. When she told Yahoo Music about the origins of "The Story of Us," it looked like Taylor Lautner was the focus, since he and Taylor had reportedly faced an awkward moment of avoiding each other at the People's Choice Awards, just weeks after breaking up.

"That was the last song that I wrote on the record, because it happened most recently. It was at an awards show, and there had been a falling out between me and this guy, and I think both of us had so much that we wanted to say, but we're sitting six seats away from each other and just fighting this silent war of, 'I don't care that you're here. I don't care that you're here.' It's so terribly, heartbreakingly awkward."

"Back to December," a wistful, apologetic tune, also looked like it focused on Lautner. She put the change in her approach to a song down to growing as a person and experiencing different emotions, saying, "up until now I haven't really felt like I really, really needed to apologize to someone and someone deserved that from me. It's just necessary. From knowing the situation and writing honestly, I can't leave that part out, and I don't think I should."

Much of the focus, however, fell on one song in particular. "Dear John" is a biting, lover-scorned tune with some of Taylor's most assured and poignant lyrics.

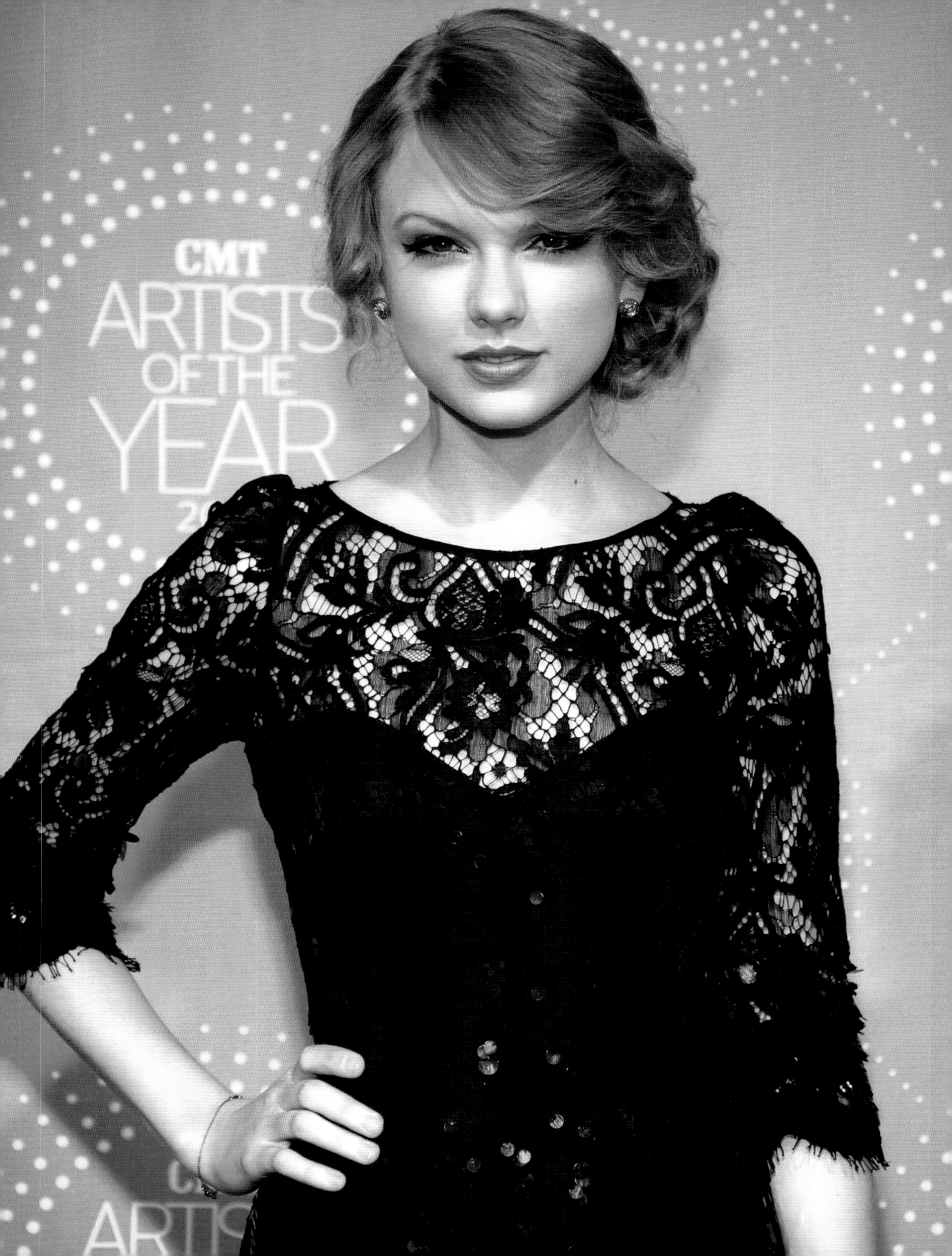
CMT
ARTISTS
OF THE
YEAR

The song is about an older man taking advantage of the feelings of a younger, more trusting and innocent girl.

The tabloid media took it that the "John" in the song was John Mayer. A few rumors had been floating about that claimed there was a romance between them ever since Taylor had worked with the notorious lothario pop star back in 2009 on "Half of My Heart," a track from his *Battle Studies* album.

When Taylor told Yahoo that "there are things that were little nuances of the relationship, little hints. And every single song is like that. Everyone will know, so I don't really have to send out e-mails on this one," the media had their evidence. After all, Mayer had tweeted that Taylor was the "Stevie Nicks to his Tom Petty" (who recorded the hit duet "Stop Draggin' My Heart Around" in 1981 and enjoyed a brief love affair). Taylor's response was a gooey, "I've been such a big fan of John for such a long time. I'm really excited about just the idea that he would even mention me in his Twitter!" to *Elle* magazine.

Once again Taylor revealed aspects of her romantic life in song, shedding light on another breakup (perhaps) on a record. For Taylor the songwriting process was vital and gave her closure. Not that Taylor was too heartbroken for long. The same day that *Speak Now* hit the stores the Internet was buzzing with rumors of her enjoying another celebrity romance, this time with the A-list Hollywood actor Jake Gyllenhaal, after they were seen together in a Brooklyn restaurant.

In November, actress Gwyneth Paltrow organized a dinner party for Jake and Taylor in London, telling *USA Today*, "I've just known Jake for a long time and he's a great guy, and Chris [Martin, of Coldplay, her husband] has a friendship with Taylor."

The new couple spent their Thanksgiving holiday in New York, where they were snapped by the paparazzi, and they had their photos taken again at Fido's coffee shop in Nashville a couple of days later. When reports emerged that Gyllenhaal had bought Taylor an expensive guitar from one of Music City's premier guitar stores, it looked as if this time Taylor might have embarked on a possibly serious relationship. Taylor was soon spotted again with Jake, in L.A. But then, suddenly, it was all over. There were no more sightings of the couple together, just reports that Jake didn't attend Taylor's twenty-first birthday party in Nashville on December 13 and that the intensely private actor and the "open book" singer had ended things amicably.

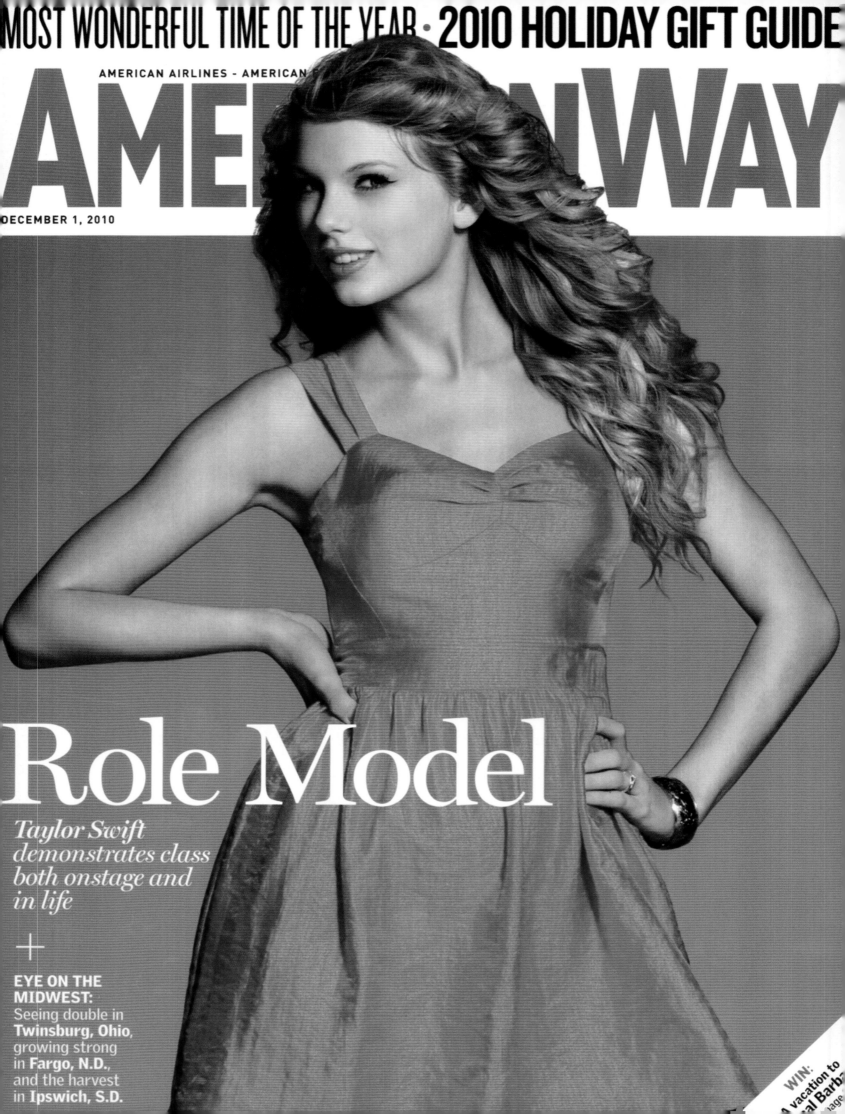

MOST WONDERFUL TIME OF THE YEAR • 2010 HOLIDAY GIFT GUIDE

AMERICAN AIRLINES - AMERICAN

AMERICANWAY

DECEMBER 1, 2010

Role Model

Taylor Swift
demonstrates class
both onstage and
in life

+

EYE ON THE
MIDWEST:
Seeing double in
Twinsburg, Ohio,
growing strong
in **Fargo, N.D.,**
and the harvest
in **Ipswich, S.D.**

WIN:
vacation to
al Barb

A BREAKUP AND A TOUR

Whatever the truth about her relationship, the publicity generated by rumors of a split from Gyllenhaal certainly didn't harm sales of *Speak Now*, which closed the year on top of the charts. *Billboard* and Nielsen Soundscan named Taylor the top-selling artist of the year, having sold more than 4.4 million albums in 2010.

Taylor was also *Billboard*'s most-played artist for the second year running as she finished on top of the Artist Airplay chart. She also dominated music's newest outlet, digital downloads, with 34 million downloads and took the top spot on *Billboard*'s Top Selling Digital Artists chart.

Forbes placed Taylor on their list of the top twenty highest-earning celebrities of 2010, entering at number nineteen with an estimated year's earnings of $45 million. As 2010 became 2011, Taylor started the new year with yet another major accolade, picking up the popular People's Choice Award for Best Country Artist from Sir Elton John.

Beginning in February 2011, Taylor's Speak Now world tour kicked off in Singapore. A major undertaking, it saw Taylor scheduled to play ninety shows in a staggering nineteen countries. Making the announcement on her second tour, Taylor was positive and upbeat about what lay ahead for her. In a press statement she said, "I'm so excited to go back out on tour again in 2011! The Fearless Tour was so much fun and even more unforgettable than I ever imagined, and I can't wait to get back out and play my new music from *Speak Now*! The fans have been so amazing, and I'm thrilled to play in new cities around the world and meet even more of my fans in 2011!"

Most of the year was taken up with touring, with only May and June free for rest and recreation at home with family. After touring across North America in late summer, Taylor Swift, it seems safe to say, is destined to continue her dramatic rise in popularity with movie roles, TV specials, and even the launch of her own perfume for Estée Lauder in her future. Where it might all end, or even if it will end, we have to wait and see, and hope that it's no time soon.

OPPOSITE AND BELOW: Taylor, a role model to her fans, on the cover and inside *American Way* magazine, November 2010.

PAGES 158–159: Taylor and her brother, Austin Swift, at the People's Choice Awards, 2011.

TIM MCGRAW

TAYLOR Swift and country superstar Tim McGraw will always be connected. It was his song "Can't Tell Me Nothing" that she had in her mind when writing her own song that was originally called "When You Think Tim McGraw." It was that song that started her on her dramatic journey to the top.

"I got the idea in math class. I was just sitting there, and I started humming this melody. I kind of related it to this situation I was in. I was dating a guy who was about to go off to college. I knew we were going to break up. So I started thinking about all the things that I knew would remind him of me. Surprisingly, the first thing that came to mind was that my favorite country artist is Tim McGraw."

The paths of Taylor and Tim would continue to cross, from a dramatic first meeting at an awards show to touring with McGraw and his wife, female country icon Faith Hill. It's little wonder that they eventually became friends and hang out together.

Tim McGraw is a country music heavyweight. He's had eleven consecutive albums debut at number one on the *Billboard* album charts and put twenty-one singles to number one on the *Billboard* country chart. He has won three Grammys, fourteen Academy of Country Music awards, eleven CMA awards, ten American Music Awards, and three People's Choice Awards. His Soul2Soul II Tour with Faith Hill is the highest-grossing in the history of country music.

Son of famous baseball star Tug McGraw Jr., Tim (b. 1967) traveled to Nashville in 1989 determined to make it as a singer. It was Mike Borchetta (father of Taylor's record company boss, Scott Borchetta) who would make McGraw's dreams a reality. A friend of a friend of Tug McGraw got a tape to Mike Borchetta at Curb Records, and after a couple of weeks of listening to it he met with Tim, and soon made him a Curb artist.

His first, self-titled album for Curb didn't do much. But being one of the more dynamic independent labels in Nashville at the time, they were patient, and the next album, *Not a Moment Too Soon*, featured a smash hit single that made McGraw a star. "Indian Outlaw" caused enough controversy (some radio station thought its Wild West–style language was offensive to Native Americans) to gain the kind of media attention a new act can't buy, and it rose to number eight on the country chart and number fifteen on the pop chart. The album went on to sell more than six million copies and made the top slot on both the country and the *Billboard* 200 charts. But concerned about the controversy that "Indian Outlaw" created, McGraw decided to meet with American Indian leaders and explain that there was no offense intended.

In 1995 Tim McGraw took a liking to fellow country singer Faith Hill In 1996, McGraw headlined the most successful country tour of the year, The Spontaneous Combustion Tour, with Faith Hill. The two stars fell in love and one night in Montana, McGraw proposed to Miss Hill in his dressing room. Faith, delighted, wrote "Yes" on his dressing room mirror. They married in Louisiana with McGraw telling *USA Today*, "I've got to be one of the luckiest guys in the world. She's incredible, one of the most down-to-earth people I've ever met in my life." The celebrity couple went on to have three daughters together: Gracie Katherine, Maggie Elizabeth, and Audrey Caroline.

Established as a major Nashville player through the 2000s, McGraw started dabbling in acting roles before playing his first lead role in the 2006 movie *Flicka*. He has also appeared in *Friday Night Lights*, *The Kingdom*, and *Four Christmases*. In the 2010 movie *Country Song*, he played a country singer alongside Oscar-winning actress Gwyneth Paltrow.

Once he was the inspiration for Taylor Swift's first single, and now he's her friend and the father of three of Taylor's biggest fans. Unsurprisingly, McGraw's not going to let anyone mess with Taylor. After the notorious Kanye West incident he told *People* magazine that he and his daughter were watching the show and excited to see Taylor win: "[My girls] were upset. But what he did do is provide a great example of how not to be, and my girls learned a big lesson. When they weren't looking I said, 'He needs an *** whoopin'!'" Taylor's got some great pals in Nashville.

OPPOSITE: Tim McGraw performing at the New Orleans Jazz and Heritage Festival in 2008.

PICTURE CREDITS

The author and publishers have made every reasonable effort to contact all copyright holders. Any errors that may have occurred are inadvertent and anyone who for any reason has not been contacted is invited to write to the publishers so that a full acknowledgement may be made in subsequent editions of this work.